THE C(OF AUTISM

Methods to Reach and Educate Children on the Autism Spectrum

Toni Flowers

Voted Teacher of the Year by
Autism Society of America

Future Horizons, Inc.

Future Horizons, Inc.
721 W. Abram Street
Arlington, Texas 76013

800-489-0727
817-277-0727
817-277-2270 (fax)

Website: www.FHautism.com
E-mail: info@FHautism.com

ISBN: 1-885477-57-0

Dedication

If you believe in yourself, it is perhaps because you had parents or loved ones like mine. Their unconditional love empowered me to believe in my child and all the children of the world.

This book is dedicated to the memory of my father, Thomas Flowers, and to the ones who will always believe—my mother, Doris Flowers, and my son, Joshua Flowers-Pasquith.

Table of Contents

Let Autism Color the Person Only After You Have a Picture of the Person to Color

Introduction

The Color of Autism is the result of almost twenty years of teaching individuals with autism. It incorporates experiences that I learned from the classroom, as well as knowledge gained from numerous conferences, visits with friends with autism, and the relationships that I have maintained with former students and their families.

Work in the field of autism is often slippery; nevertheless, I would like to share a few constants that I have found over the years.

- There is not one way to teach, reach, or live with a person with autism. It is an individual journey, and each person with autism needs individual goals.
- The educational journey of a person with autism does not follow a printed map. The journey takes detours, and you need to allow these detours—sometimes following, sometimes leading, but never giving up.
- Your vision of the finish line will not be the same vision as the vision of the person with autism.
- You need to focus on the individual's ability, not the disability.
- Many things I have learned about autism are not universal, but they are pertinent to one person's autism.
- Nothing is wasted on a person with autism. It is better to try something than to do nothing. You can step back and adjust later.
- I have found that the more I discover about autism, the more there is to learn. As I fill in the blanks, the canvas grows larger.

Open *The Color of Autism* and use what works. Tweak the suggestions. Refine them. Rework them. Learn to continually look beyond the autism and see the child's individual strengths and weaknesses, interests, personalities, hopes, and dreams.

Respect people with autism as individuals and challenge them to do their best. You will not be disappointed.

Self Portrait
14 year old

Chapter One

Challenges and Expectations

The Child with Autism Can Learn!

Do not focus on any old expectations. Have high expectations. **Don't leave home without them!**

Expectations are critical to the education of any child, but they are especially so for a child with autism. So many people are mystified by autism and believe that there are things that the child cannot do (and will never do) because of the disorder.

The truth is that a person with autism can learn to do almost anything anyone else can. Individuals with autism, however, do not learn some of the givens that we learn just by being in an environment. Incidental learning does not always happen for people with the disorder. Therefore, those with autism sometimes need to learn things that we do not traditionally see as lessons. Playing, socializing, and behaving in a manner appropriate for the situation are a few that come to mind.

The way people with autism learn, and the rate at which they learn, can be dramatically different from individuals without autism. Developing a skill can take much longer for those with the disorder.

First, however, the expectation has to be that the person with autism can and will learn a skill. The challenge comes in how to teach.

My friend Pam Kuhn and I have shared many students with autism, and we also share in our strong belief in the abilities of those children and the importance of high expectations. Pam wrote the following:

> As a teacher of children with autism, I have found that having high expectations of my students and working with their strengths encourages them to excel in ways that they may not have done otherwise.
>
> Often, children with disabilities are given different, watered-down rules. There can be many different reasons for this, such as misunderstandings, misconceptions, or underestimations.
>
> Usually, the decision to make few demands is made with good intentions. Whatever the reason, when a child with autism is not given the opportunity to rise to a challenge, no matter how difficult, it is the child who loses.
>
> Children with autism can learn. You need to challenge them as much as, or more than, any other child. Self-esteem is hard to measure, but once you witness a person master a difficult task after months of struggle, you realize that confidence in one's ability is critical as a foundation for further learning. In not giving a person the chance to make mistakes and learn from mistakes, the opportunity to learn and grow diminishes immensely.

Why should individuals with autism not learn to follow rules? To not expect this of them minimizes them as human beings. Their future is as precious as any other person's.

It can take a long time for people with autism to learn the basics. Limiting children by predetermining what they can and cannot learn ultimately slows them down and reduces their chances for success.

I taught one child, Billy, whose mother had difficulty with him at home due to his aggression toward the family and himself. Unfortunately, there were few rules that the mother expected

Billy and his brother to follow. The mother said she did not make rules because she wanted her children to be happy. She also saw Billy in the spotlight of his autism and did not expect him capable of learning rules. She felt that to impose rules on him was useless and would only make him "unhappy."

However, when things got out of control at home, no one was happy. As frustrated as the mother became, she still did not see Billy as capable of learning and following rules.

In addition to having low expectations of Billy's behavior, the mother had low academic expectations. Billy was attending a kindergarten class, in addition to his special education class, and was doing well—especially academically. He continued to learn and behave at school, but he kept up the old patterns at home. This puzzled his parents. How could he behave one way at school and another way at home?

One of the things I strongly encourage my parents to do is to keep a daily notebook and write notes to me as often as possible. In turn, I write daily notes on behavior, extracurricular activities, academic gains, etc. These notebooks are invaluable in fine tuning the child's day. The more information you have about what has happened between home and school, the better.

In one of her notes, Billy's mother wrote: "In the name of autism, Billy gets away with a lot." I saw this as a bridge of hope for Billy and his family. I felt that Billy's mother was beginning to see beyond Billy's autism. This encouraged me, and I wrote her at length on my view of expectations. What follows is an excerpt from that letter.

Dear Mary,

Today I am going to write to you about how I view expectations.

If you expect Billy to be aggressive, he will be.

If you expect that Billy can't learn not to be aggressive, he won't.

If you expect autism to be the reason he doesn't (not "can't") control himself, he won't.

If you believe that autism is the reason he can't control his actions, he'll continue not to control them.

If you expect Billy to learn, he will.

Autism does not prevent Billy from learning! Billy may learn in ways that are different from other children. It may take him longer to learn something. But he can and does learn.

He learns things that we purposefully teach him, and he learns things we don't want him to learn. It seems to me that Billy has learned that he can do as he pleases at home. He has learned to get attention by being aggressive. He has learned that a tantrum will get his needs met nicely.

To turn this behavior around, you must have the expectation that he can and will learn what he needs to learn to be a positive member of your family.

At school, Billy is expected to learn and have confidence in his ability to grasp new things, and he does. At school, Billy is expected to refrain from aggression against others, and he rarely shows aggression.

When you expect nothing, you will get nothing. When you expect the worst, you will get the worst. When you tolerate aggression and blame it on autism, he will use aggression because it is what you have come to expect from him.

Turn that around and expect good behavior and increased knowledge. Consistency in your expectations is very important. Billy can see that he can get away with things when you don't follow set rules at home. Make rules and help him to follow them.

If you have expectations at home for behavior and learning and are consistent in your approach, you won't be disappointed in the changes you will see in Billy.

Billy's mother replied that she would try to make changes at home. She did change a few things, but it was not until several months later, when things began to really get out of control, that she started to get serious about her expectations. The mother began regular visits to the school. She saw firsthand how Billy behaved in this environment. He went to a regular class and had few tantrums. His academic skills continued to grow.

Billy's mother realized that he was indeed a different child at home. She also realized that the family's expectations of Billy were different than the expectations at school.

The mother started slowly by imposing one rule at a time. From that point on, we kept open communication through daily notes, phone calls, home, and school visits about which methods were working and which were not. We worked to best facilitate consistency between home and school.

When the family started to see beyond Billy's autism and view him as a child that could learn to follow rules, Billy's behavior began improving. Billy will always have difficulty, and he will always have autism, but he is no longer getting away with mayhem in the name of autism.

Cat by
6 year old

Chapter Two

So Many Words – So Little Time

Change Your Way of Communicating

The world is a verbal place, and for individuals with autism, that can spell:

C-O-N-F-U-S-I-O-N

Many individuals with autism have difficulty to one degree or another sorting through the verbal jungle that shapes and defines our world.

- We "normals" are a verbal lot.
- We talk to give information.
- We talk to receive information.
- We talk for social purposes.
- Our words can make people laugh.
- Our words can make people cry.
- We say things we don't mean.
- We ask questions when we don't really care about the answer.
- We talk to ourselves.
- We say the same thing in multiple ways, sometimes within the same conversation.
- We talk fast.
- We talk with our mouths full of food.
- We talk when other people are talking.
- We talk with clichs.
- We babble.
- We mumble.
- We grumble and groan.
- We leave sentences unfinished.
- We ramble on.
- We rant.
- We rave.
- We use our entire bodies to punctuate our words.

Individuals with autism have problems processing the spoken word to varying degrees. They may have difficulty integrating the verbal information they receive, and they probably have a difficult time transferring the words into meaning and then into action.

The most well-meaning, sociable, "normal" individual could be a person with autism's worst nightmare. If you have ever traveled in a foreign country and really needed information to get to your destination, order some dinner, or find help in an emergency, you might come close to experiencing what the person with autism feels to some degree or another. The person with autism experiences this frustration, anxiety, and sheer helplessness on a daily basis. You can get on a plane and return home to your native tongue when things get overwhelming. A person with autism does not have this option.

The range of difficulty a person with autism experiences with language is probably as vast and diverse as the autism spectrum itself. With practice, successes, and reflection, however, you become adept at gearing your conversation to many different levels of understanding.

The rules that govern our everyday communication do not always apply to the individual with autism. The following scenario between a teacher and a student with autism illustrates this.

> The teacher asks for the student's lunch money. She says, with all good intentions, "Give me your lunch money. You are going to be really hungry if you don't give me your money. Where is your money? Did your mother send it today, or did she forget it again? We're having hamburgers today, and I know that you love hamburgers. If you give me the lunch money right now, I will let you play on the computer after lunch."

> The child does not respond. Immediately, the teacher says in a louder voice, with exasperation dripping from each word, "OK, it is almost lunchtime. We need your money. All of

the other children gave me their money. If you don't give me the money, the other kids will go hungry, and they will be mad at you."

The teacher gestures towards the closet where the student's book bag is. The classroom assistant is by the closet. She jumps into the mix. "Come here. Your lunch money is over here. Hurry up. I know that you are hungry. Yum, yum," she says, rubbing her stomach. "I'll get you dessert if you come on. I think it is apple pie, or is it cookies? Well, no matter, I'll get you both. Be a good boy. Come on."

The teacher is still instructing at the other end of the classroom. The child does not respond in the appropriate manner. The teacher throws up her hands, declares the student stubborn, and goes to the closet to get the lunch money. The child flops to the floor and begins to whine and bite on his hand. Teacher says, "I am going to count to ten, and you had better be up and in line. It is time for lunch, Mister."

The assistant takes over and counts to ten for the teacher. Okay, into time out. They are going to lunch without you." The class leaves. The confused child is in the corner with the assistant standing over him. The assistant tells the child that he should have listened the first time, and it is time to stop being so stubborn.

The following are suggestions that could make life simpler and more productive for everyone when talking to a person with autism:

1. **The Buddy System.** I am sure that you have heard the phrase, "Don't go swimming without a buddy." Many people with autism need a buddy to go along with the spoken word. The buddy can be a visual cue like an object, a picture, or the written word.

2. **Is It a Bird or a Plane?** Many people use their arms and hands when talking as if about to be airborne. A very lively conversationalist with arms going like a windmill can be

confusing to those of us without autism. For a person with autism, who experiences difficulty processing auditory input and body language, all of this fluttering of arms and hands and swaying of the body does not punctuate the meaning of the words, but instead becomes an irrelevant distraction. Keep yourself grounded when speaking to individuals with autism.

3. **Goo Goo – Gaa Gaa.** You may need to limit the amount of language you use when speaking to people with autism. Think of this as a courtesy, as well as a teaching tool. This does not mean, however, that you talk in that high, squeaky voice that some people use with babies and turn your words into clipped versions of their former selves. This way of talking is demeaning and counter-productive to instruction. It also hurts the student's self-esteem.

4. **Louder Is Not Better.** Have you ever had a heated conversation with someone who felt frustrated when you did not understand what he was saying, so he says it again in a louder voice? Louder voices do not negate confusion or clear up any misunderstandings. Many individuals with autism have an aversion to loud noises. Calm and controlled conversation is better.

5. **Don't Change Horses in the Middle of the Stream.** Rewording a phrase several times will not increase understanding. Use the same language that you used the first time. If anything, use less of the same language. Do not confuse the person by changing words in an effort to make him understand.

6. **Speak Slowly to Allow Time for Processing.** Say what you need to say. Take a deep breath. Breathe in for about eight seconds; breathe out for eight seconds. This not only gives the person with autism time to process what you are saying, it will also calm you. If you need to repeat, do so slowly, calmly, and breathe in and breathe out. Do not act

frustrated, disgusted, or angry. If you need to repeat, do so with patience, understanding, and respect for the person.

7. **Buff Your Idea.** Abstract language and slang may confuse the person with autism. Throw out all the extraneous bits of information and colorful adjectives. People with autism may take things literally. Think about what you want to convey and do so without all the extras.

8. **Who Is the Student Anyway?** Do not give up, throw your hands in the air, and do the task for the student. You do not need to practice the task—the student does. In doing for a child, you take away that teachable moment. When you do for people instead of helping students through the process of doing for themselves, you have told them loud and clear, "I do not think you can do this. I do not have faith in your learning abilities."

When you feel yourself getting ready to do something for children that they need to learn for themselves, stop and reflect! Take a child through the request using the same language that you used the first time. Give meaning to the words. Show them, as well as tell them, what the words mean.

9. **Actions Speak Louder than Words.** There are times when it is effective not to use words at all. Demonstrate what you want the child to do. You can add words later.

10. **Listen to Me, Me, and Me.** When one person talks to the student with autism, other people in the room should be quiet and allow the student to focus on what the person speaking is saying.

11. **Fire!!!!** Stay calm and speak in calm tones. If the person with autism is having problems processing what you are saying because you are saying it hysterically, he will likely miss the verbal message but pick up on the hysteria (whether there is anything to get excited about or not).

12. **The Final Word.** Do not let the last word of the sentence be the part you do not want the student to do. For example, the teacher says, "Walk, don't run." The student may only hear the word "run" and do exactly that.

The following students show some of *The Color of Autism.*

The Color of Autism: **Derek**

Derek had played with the blocks for at least an hour. He sat lost in his towers and tunnels. Paul approached and sat down across from Derek and his structures. Derek grunted but did not say anything. Paul swept his hand across the nearest tower and sent it flying across the floor. Derek grunted again. Paul reached over and took a block out of Derek's hand.

"Good grief, Derek! Stand up for yourself," the teacher called. Derek looked at Paul, got on his hands and knees, and pushed himself up. He stood there, perfectly compliant to the teacher's command.

When a teacher adjusts the way of communicating to take into consideration the student's specific learning style, the student has a better chance of learning. Once you have found a workable system to help the person with autism communicate, think of it as a starting point—not as a finish line.

Revisiting the lunchroom disaster the teacher should build into the student's day a time to bring lunch money, notebooks, etc., to her or him. A good time to do this is first thing in the morning before the students hang up their book bags. When lunchtime approaches, the child does not have to get money but only a lunch ticket from a designated place. The ticket is the visual "buddy" cue that accompanies the request to get ready for lunch.

The teacher only has to say, "Time for lunch. Line up." Give the student time to process and respond. Repeat the request, using the same language. If the student does not respond, the teacher can tell and show him what to do. Language is limited and concise, yet respectful. Others in the room need to stay quiet so that the people with autism hear only one voice.

The teacher has eliminated the confusing verbiage. Expectations are clear and concise. This process will become part of the person's daily routine, giving him or her control and understanding over one more piece of the day.

The Color of Autism: Fred

Fred's job was to sweep the cafeteria floor every day after lunch. Fred would sweep and then adjust his underwear. Sweep. Stop. Adjust. Sweep. Stop. Adjust. The teacher noticed what Fred was doing and realized that it would take him forever to clean the floor and get back to class. "Fred," she said, "Just sweep. We'll fix your underwear when you have finished sweeping." Fred continued to sweep, but he took one hand off the broom, adjusted the underwear, and kept the broom going with the other hand. Now he was sweeping and adjusting. Straws and bits of food were going in every direction. One-handed sweeping really does not do the job. The teacher watched Fred for a few minutes and then said, "Fred, use both hands." Fred looked relieved as he dropped the broom and put both hands to work adjusting the underwear.

The Color of Autism: Alex

Alex was typing his daily letter home. He stopped and seemed unable to add anything else. "Alex," I said, "Tell me four things you did at school today." Alex looked as if he were pondering his day. I busied myself elsewhere. When I came back to the computer, I saw what he had typed:

Dear Toni,

1   2   3   4

I tried again. "Alex, just write me a letter." When I came back to check on him, I saw that Alex had done exactly that:

Dear Toni,

G

The Color of Autism: Mickey

Mickey was progressing in the third grade. He had an even temperament as long as he was prepared for any changes that might occur in his day. His schedule had made a tremendous difference for him in this area.

Both teacher and students were perplexed when on October 1, Mickey began to get agitated. He cried easily and was generally unpleasant. Nothing seemed to help. No one could think of anything to make Mickey's day better.

The mystery was solved when one of the students pulled out the dress-up trunk and began trying on masks. Mickey saw the masks and howled. The teacher thought that perhaps the masks frightened Mickey, so she took him from the classroom. They sat in his quiet area right outside the room. The teacher asked question after question, but Mickey only howled louder. Nothing worked, so the teacher suggested that Mickey go home until he calmed down. Mickey raced to the computer to write his "Dear Mom" letter, which was the last thing he did each day.

Dear Mom;

I went to gym. I went to music. I had a hotdog for lunch. I am sad. I want to go where Halloween is.

Love,
Mickey

The teacher and students went to the calendar area. They put the Halloween sticker on the 31st of October. Each student took turns counting the days until Halloween. They told stories about their favorite Halloween. They made individual calendars with a Halloween sticker on the 31st of October. Mickey stopped crying and resumed smiling. He started each day with, "I will go to where Halloween is in 20 days, 19 days" On the 31st, Mickey entered the classroom and said, "I am where Halloween is." When Halloween was safely behind, the class began the same process for Thanksgiving, Christmas, and then for every holiday or event in which Mickey expressed an interest.

I always think of Mickey around my birthday and tell myself, "I don't want to go where my birthday is this year."

The Color of Autism: Ken

One of Ken's goals was to cross the street independently. Our school was on a busy city street. Every day I took Ken to the curb and instructed him to look both ways. I then would ask him if he saw a car. Ken would look both ways and then say, "Yes." I quickly realized that he was spotting cars that were parked along the street. I tried again and reworded my question. I told him to look both ways and tell me if he saw a moving car.

Ken looked both ways and replied, "Yes." I was baffled for a second, but then I realized that he had indeed spotted a car, but it was moving away from us and was not a danger.

Self Portrait
9 year old

Chapter Three

I Never Met a Person with Autism I Didn't Like

The Importance of Teacher-Student Bonding

Bonding is a crucial part of the learning process in any student-teacher relationship. That special give-and-take between the teacher and student can tremendously impact the quality of learning.

The area of personal relationships is particularly difficult for individuals with autism, and the process of forming a relationship can be slow and frustrating. Many times the relationship is forming, but it takes such a crooked path that the teacher might be unaware of it.

The signals that such a relationship is on the horizon might not be apparent, so a teacher could assume that bonding with a person with autism is impossible. With such an assumption, the teacher will miss real opportunities to foster the growth of a very special relationship. However, if a teacher realizes that the potential is always there, and if she or he is patient, watches for even the tiniest signal, and offers encouragement, the relationship will form.

A relationship with a child with autism is all the more precious because it can take so many unexpected detours and be so long in coming. However, it is definitely worth the wait.

When a person with autism acknowledges you, accepts you, and loves you, the love is pure and simple. There is no other love quite like it. It cannot be manipulated or forced. The love is totally without terms or conditions.

Many of life's lessons that might otherwise elude a person with autism may present themselves and be experienced, dealt with, and learned from during the process of forming and maintaining a relationship. Individuals with autism do go through life's emotional experiences; however, they do so with different perceptions, in different time frames, and with a very different frame of reference. All of this can be baffling to a person who is trying to form a relationship.

Bonding can take time, and the student and teacher form relationships in ways unique to their situation and individual personalities. The bonding process, and its positive outcome, are crucial to the child's chances of forming relationships in the future. The learning process needs to continue while a relationship is building; however, once the child with autism accepts you and knows that you accept him or her, learning often takes a leap forward.

The Color of Autism: **Charles**

Charles was a stocky, little five-year-old with a set jaw, scowl, and the neck of a football player. He did not talk; instead, he screamed in rage and glared at everyone and everything, with the exception of food. When he saw food, he would hurl his mighty little body into any obstacle that stood in his way. At night, Charles' mother had to be alert to the sounds of him raiding the refrigerator. He would empty the frozen food onto the floor and eat bits and pieces, leaving the bulk to defrost and spoil. If his mother discovered him and tried to get him to stop and go back to bed, Charles would use his head as a battering ram and butt her in the stomach as hard as he could. He once set the house on fire in the middle of the night. Fortunately, his mother smelled the smoke, thus avoiding disaster.

Our first goal for Charles was to get him to sit in his chair. If we put Charles in his chair, he would tumble out, kicking and screaming. I tried placing him back in the chair with this directive: "You will sit." Charles would answer with a scream and hurl his body back onto the floor.

Charles' obsession with food made snack time a perfect lesson for sitting. I started by announcing to Charles, "You will sit. If you do not sit, no snack." Charles did not take me (or anyone else) seriously at first. He had five years of ruling by the wrath of his little temper. His chair went one direction, and Charles' little body came flying across the table to procure the snack. My assistant would take over the snack, and I would remove Charles to a position where he would have to watch the snack from afar.

Progress was slow, and I went home exhausted each night. Sometimes, I thought that it would be best to give in and not expect Charles to sit. Then one night, I thought about all of the things that Charles may never do that I knew he could do. It was assumed that Charles would never be able to learn to write his name or to learn his colors, numbers, letters, and other kindergarten skills, have a job or be a contributing member of society. Therefore, when Charles entered the school the next day, the battle for his future began anew.

Charles was a small child with a will of iron and a determination that I could not help but admire. It was imperative that he master that first important step of sitting so that we could begin to channel his talents before he was a bigger, stronger, more determined ten-year-old and then a twenty-one-year-old (with no school to fill his days).

I learned after my first few idealistic years in working with children with autism that there is not one dramatic breakthrough. Progress is slow and choppy, with results that sometimes creep up on you. Charles fought courageously to hold onto his old, proven patterns of behavior, but he was losing.

Charles was forming the concepts of a new way to do things: a gentler way, a simpler and more satisfactory way. He began to respond to praise for the many small things he did that he had never focused on before.

There were days when Charles sat for a while, but there were days when Charles still fought that chair with all his might. I vividly remember one of his fighting days. It was the day I wanted to walk away and never look back.

The day was a half-day with no lunch. Snack was the last thing on the agenda. The structure of the day unsettled Charles. As we got ready to have our snack, he tumbled to the floor with the chair falling on top of him. My assistant took over snack duties, and I took over Charles. I helped him turn his chair upright and sit. Time and time again, he threw himself one way and his chair another. Time and time again, I helped him pick up his little chair and sit.

Finally, it was time to leave. Charles had not stopped growling and fighting the chair. All the other children went about the business of going home. They put on their jackets, packed their papers, and went out the door. Charles no longer wanted a snack. His mind was on one thing, and one thing only—going home. He gave a roar and hurled himself against me, sending us both tumbling to the floor.

I heard my skirt rip as I struggled to get my arms and legs wrapped around Charles before my entire outfit was in shreds. I had him temporarily restrained when the principal walked in, stopped, stared, and exclaimed, "Oh, dear!" She then regained her composure and politely asked if there was anything she could do to assist me. I was breathing in short little gasps, but I managed to smile, reach behind me with one hand, upright the little chair, and lift Charles up and plop him on the chair. "First you sit, then you go home." I could tell the principal was looking at my ripped skirt, but I kept my eyes riveted on Charles. "Really, we are fine," I told her. "Just a lesson in sitting."

For one full minute Charles sat. It seemed like an hour. I gave a sigh of relief and told him to get his book bag and go home.

Progress was faster after that day. Charles rarely missed a snack. He sat during the morning group and began exploring crayons, pencils, and paper.

Charles began saying more words, but my favorite was when he called me "Toie." Shortly after that, he began saying all the children's names, and his mother said that he would lie in bed at night and recite all of our names until he fell asleep.

Charles quickly learned that language was a powerful tool. One day, when it was Charles' turn to shake my hand and say good morning, he squeezed my hand and got very close to my face and said, "I luf you Toie, go play please?" Charles played.

Charles moved on to another school. I was visiting it one day, and I looked for Charles. He looked up from his desk, and our eyes met. He got up and came towards me saying, "Toie, Toie Toie," and I said, "Charles, Charles, Charles." We hugged, not having much of a conversation as conversation goes, but we had managed to say a lot. As I thanked the teacher and got ready to leave, she suggested Charles and I might want to visit a little longer. I told her our visit had been just right, and I did not want to disrupt his day. I looked at Charles, and he smiled and waved.

Five years after I met Charles, I took him to a lunch buffet. The little boy with the eating compulsion did a great job. He went through the line, piling food on his plate without spilling a thing. I wanted to tell everyone in the restaurant that they were witnesses to a wonderful moment, but as my pride was swelling, Charles snatched a chicken leg off a woman's plate. The woman gave us a dirty look as I removed the leg from Charles' plate and mumbled apologies. I nudged Charles and had him say, "Sorry."

I recently received a Christmas card from Charles and his family, and I couldn't help noticing with pride that Charles had signed his own name in cursive.

The Color of Autism: **Patrick**

Patrick came into my classroom with oral abilities. At first, he described everything as "new": my new arm, my new mom, my new pencil, etc. Then Patrick added "almost." For example, "I almost ate the new cookie," or "I almost missed my new mom."

Patrick moved his chair next to mine in our circle, and it remained there all year. Patrick did aerobic exercises next to me each morning. When I was absent, or even left the room, Patrick demanded that I return. When I did not appear, he would accuse people of having an attitude problem. When we walked down the hall we made "Pat tracks." He loved video games and made wooden blocks into the video game, Tetrus®.

When a new boy moved into our class, Patrick was furious. He said, "There are too many Toni's boys already." When that statement did not get results, and the new boy remained, Patrick stood up and announced, "You have five seconds to tell him to talk, or he's out of here."

One day I was absent, and Patrick spent recess howling and demanding my return. When the substitute tried to console him, Patrick demanded, "Get me to Toni's room." When I was not there, Patrick howled louder. The substitute tried to distract him by telling him that he was a smart little boy. Patrick sobbed harder and corrected her, "No, I am a sad little boy."

I told Patrick goodbye for the summer. As I knelt to give this six-year-old wizard a hug, he said, "Excuse me, excuse me Toni, but the colors got mixed up, the flavors got mixed up." He pulled a secret Kool-Aid decoder from his pocket and presented it to me.

The Color of Autism: **Allen**

Allen came into my room as a kindergartner. He said, "Op, Op," and looked through his fingers, making triangles and circles in front of his face.

When it was time to play, Allen held a small toy to his face and wiggled it around, sometimes still using his fingers as a picture frame. He sometimes sucked his thumb and twisted his ear so that it stayed tucked into itself. My son, who was a big fan of Allen's, nicknamed him old "Tuck and Suck."

When it was time to do seat work, Allen would get on his knees at his desk, twiddle his pencil, and say, "Op, Op." He ignored the work in front of him unless he was physically guided through it. He did not actively participate in group activities. If I patted him in praise, he would pull away. If I attempted to hug him, he would leave.

Allen made a little progress as the school year slipped by. He briefly looked at books. He would hold a pencil and trace lines. He would color a picture. But if left alone at his desk, he still would get on his knees, twiddle his pencil, and say, "Op, Op."

Allen returned to my class the following fall. There were a few subtle differences. He gave me fleeting eye contact when I talked to him. He followed simple directions. Occasionally, I caught a fleeting smile when I teased him. He began to talk, saying everyone's name in the group. He shook hands and said "Good morning" to each of us. Allen still sat at his desk and twiddled his pencil some, but he was beginning to work independently, and we did not hear "Op, Op."

One day I was working with another student when I saw Allen get out of his chair. I watched him as he looked on each shelf of the bookcase and finally located a pair of scissors. He went back to his desk and began working with a satisfied look on his face. I was so proud of him. He was starting to problem solve for himself. This was a big step.

Allen always placed his chair by mine in the morning group. When we were out of the classroom, Allen was always within touching distance of me. He now tolerated little pats and hugs. He had begun to use sentences. He began saying my name softly and always twice: "Toni, Toni." Before winter break, it was very apparent that Allen had a crush on his teacher like many other first grade students. However, unlike other first graders, it had taken Allen a considerable amount of time to develop his crush and then express it. He did not give me little scraps of paper with "I love you'" written on them. He didn't draw hearts on his artwork and present it to me. Actually, Allen took a more direct approach. If anyone attempted to take Allen's spot by my side in the morning circle, Allen would pull him or her from the chair and resume his place. Eventually, he began expressing his ownership of the teacher verbally. After he had physically removed someone from my side, he would announce, "Mine," meaning me.

Allen spent an entire art period molding my name in clay. On one memorable day, Allen went to the calendar and read the days of the week. Thinking that he had memorized them in order, we mixed them up. He read them again. He then read everyone's name, smiled, and sat down. Allen had shown us that he could read. Like many other children with autism, Allen had probably been reading for some time without anyone being aware of it.

Allen and I explored art together during our weekly library time. There was a drab painting by the book exchange table. Allen would sit through slide shows, film strips, and stories, giving part of his attention to the task at hand while he kept glancing at the painting. When class was over, Allen would look at me pleadingly. I would wait until he used language to get his needs met. Allen and I would then stand in front of the painting and discuss it. He usually built on our discussion of the previous week.

Our discussion went like this:
Allen: "Man?"
Toni: "No, it is a woman. See, she is wearing a dress."
Allen: "It is a woman. Door?"
Toni: "No, it is a window."
Allen: "Flowers?"
Toni: "Yes, those are flowers."

Allen always found new things to discuss each week.

One night Allen came home with me to have a sleepover with my son Joshua. Allen was Josh's favorite kid in my class that year. Josh made a campground on his bedroom floor with two sleeping bags. He chatted away while Allen sat in the corner twiddling a toy in front of his face. Josh crawled into his sleeping bag, giving Allen a demonstration of how to stick in his feet and legs, zip up the bag, etc. Allen stood up and stepped carefully over Josh and the sleeping bags. He walked straight to Josh's bed, pulled back the covers, crawled in, and pulled up the covers. Allen did not say a word, but the expression on his face was one of, "OK, you people may sleep on the floor, but at my house we sleep in beds."

I was about to intervene and suggest that Allen experience this make-believe "campout," but Josh said, "It's okay, let him sleep there." Allen and Josh had worked it out for themselves. Allen smiled, turned over, and went to sleep.

As the school year went on, Allen began participating in all parts of our day. He talked more at home and school. He used longer sentences with fewer cues. He expanded his crush on me to my assistant, Dee. When I was not at school, Allen was satisfied if Dee were there.

Allen's third school year began. He bounded off the bus, all smiles, saying, "Toni, Toni. Hi, Toni, Toni." He looked curiously at the tiny kindergarten children who had joined our class. He looked upset as I calmed them, cuddled them, reprimanded them, and began the slow bonding process with a new group of students. Allen moved his chair up to mine in the circle.

On the second week of school, another student joined our class. The enrollment had hit the top with Allen being the oldest of the group. It was time for him to move to the intermediate group.

I tried to prepare Allen for what was going to happen. We went through rehearsals, pictures, and discussions, but when the day came, and I took him to the new room (just two doors down and with a familiar teacher), the surprise and hurt on his face broke my heart. I could tell that nothing I had done had prepared him for what he felt at that moment. I walked out of the room, trying to act nonchalant, and left him with his new teacher and classmates. I'll never forget the look of hurt and betrayal that was on his face that day.

There was a bright side to this sad day. It was a learning experience for Allen. He was learning that you have to move on when the time is right. You have to accept it, live with it, and keep growing.

At first, Allen refused to accept the change. He would come to my room every morning and hang up his coat in the spot where his nametag had been. He would look at me, waiting for me to tell him what he already knew. I would escort him to his classroom, and he would give me an angry look as I left.

All this occurred early in the school year. It took Allen until the end of the school year to speak to me or allow a hug. I really missed hearing, "Toni, Toni."

Although Allen's move caused him sadness, it also allowed him to grow. Allen's difficulty in separating from Dee and me was bittersweet because this is the very thing many children with autism all too often do not experience in the first place.

The Color of Autism: **Michael**

I attended a National Autism Society banquet several years ago when a young man approached me and said, "Hi, Toni." He looked vaguely familiar, but I could not place him. Another adult came up and introduced him as Michael, a member of my group at camp several years ago.

He had grown a few feet since then, and I had reason not to recognize him, but I also had changed. At camp, I was usually in shorts and a tee shirt with my hair pulled back. On this particular night I was dressed up—I had on makeup, my hair was totally different, and I was wearing glasses. Yet Michael recognized me instantly.

The Color of Autism: **Donnie**

Donnie was a cute little kindergartner with curly hair and a beautiful face. He loved to draw and turned all of his favorite cartoon characters into similarly looking round figures that somehow captured the essence of the characters.

Donnie was in my class for two years before he moved to a neighboring school district. I observed him in his new school a year later, and he greeted me and then appeared to ignore me.

Eight years later, Donnie telephoned me. "Hi, Toni Flowers. This is Donnie. You have high-heel shoes? You live on Central Avenue." This is inappropriate phone banter for most high school-age students, but Donnie had autism, and I was intrigued that he had called me after so many years.

"I want to see you," he said. "I will come to see you now. I will hug you." He repeated my address a few times. I told him that I was getting ready to leave and would not be at home if he came to my house. I did not think there was a chance that he would actually find me.

I really was leaving, so I continued to get ready. Forty minutes later there was a knock on the door. It was Donnie. He was much bigger than the last time I had seen him. I let him in, and he dove at me for a hug. I hugged him politely and pushed him back. I tried to find out why he had called me, how he had found me, etc. But Donnie did not come to chat. He was on a mission and that mission involved hugs. I declined the hugs and kisses and asked him how he had managed to get to my house. He said that he had taken a bus. That amazed me, and I tried to find out how many transfers he had to make, but he was determined to have physical contact. I dropped the normal reunion talk and became the teacher. I put physical distance between us and told him no. "No hugs! No kisses!" He came towards me determined to get a hug. I guided him to the door and told him he had to go because I was getting ready to leave. I offered him a ride home. He declined, saying that he liked the bus. He made no effort to get back into the house. I watched him walk to the bus stop and wait. He looked back several times and waved.

I called Donnie's house and expressed my concerns to his mother. His mother said he would be fine. He had memorized bus routes and traveled all over the city. I asked if he had spoken about me over the years. She said that he had not. I thanked her, and we hung up. That was six years ago, and I have not heard from Donnie since.

The Color of Autism: **Jen**

Jen was a twelve-year-old, hearing-impaired child that had just been diagnosed with autism. I was asked to do a home program for her. She had become increasingly aggressive and had just injured her grandmother with a carefully placed punch to the stomach. This assault seemed to be the last straw because Jen's parents were investigating alternative living arrangements for her.

Jen had some unusual hobbies, such as pouring water over the light bulbs or flooding the bathroom, usually in the middle of the night. Like many other children with autism, she did not require much sleep, so she liked to roam at night and play in the water.

With the aid of Jen's teacher, we placed picture charts around the house to help Jen follow her basic routines. Jen responded to the charts, and things became more manageable at home. We then tackled the community. Jen needed to learn essential living and social skills.

Jen's classroom teacher would accompany Jen and me (and sometimes her younger brother and my son) on excursions to museums, parks, malls, bowling alleys, and even the movies.

Jen had a very unsociable habit of shoving people as hard as she could and then running away. One day we were in a craft store looking for a hobby for Jen. Jen ran around an aisle, came up behind me, and shoved me as hard as she could. I fell into the display rack, and things fell everywhere. I grabbed Jen before she could dart away and push some unsuspecting shopper. I made Jen pick up every single item. It was a struggle, and I'm sure it wasn't pretty. Several shoppers stopped and stared at us, but I persisted until the floor was clean.

When we got to the car, I used a combination of Jen's picture communication book and sign language to tell her that if she hit or pushed on our trip, the trip was over. She would have to go home, and I would leave her there.

On our next trip, Jen started out exceptionally sweet. We looked at her communication book, and I explained again what would happen if she pushed or hit. The trip went along smoothly until Jen suddenly clobbered me. I took her arm firmly, marched her to the car, and drove her home. At the door I went over her rules again, letting her know that I would be back next week.

I had established limits, and I was comfortable that Jen understood the limits and was going to honor them. A new relationship began to form between us, based on mutual respect and understanding.

Jen only pushed me one other time. It was an "I'm going to see if she really means this" push, and it was a good one. We were in a department store. Pushing our shopping cart aside, I pulled Jen out of the store. We had spent considerable time shopping, and the cart was full of items we had selected.

Jen was very quiet on the way home and even gave me a dirty look when I left without giving her a hug. She never hit or pushed me again. She even looked at me differently after that. I do not think that she had ever been treated like a real person. Jen had so many problems that everyone had let her labels take the blame for her behavior. She was hearing-impaired, had autism, and if that were not enough, she also had a rare physical disability. Jen also had spunk and dignity, and I am sure she knew that she was being treated differently than other people. This angered and frustrated her. The expectations placed on her were too low. No one had ever given her the responsibility to control her temper, and no one had taught her options to pushing and hitting. When the expectation was placed on Jen that she would not (and could not) hit others, and there was a direct consequence placed upon her, she rose to the occasion. I gave her control over whether we continued our weekly trips.

Jen's brother did not treat her very nicely at first. He called her stupid and acted as if she were a burden. He watched me with interest week after week as Jen and I squabbled, negotiated, and finally came to an agreement on how she would behave. I expected things from her, did not tolerate certain behaviors, and gave her many different responsibilities. I watched Jen's brother's behavior toward his sister slowly change. Soon there was a new gentleness to his actions and a certain protectiveness.

Even though he was several years younger than Jen, he began assuming the role of big brother. He started showing pride in her accomplishments.

My favorite memory of our times together was when Jen and I were driving along, and I was listening to a lively song on the radio. I glanced over at Jen. She was playing with her koosh ball, locked away in her deaf, autistic world.

I wanted to share the music with her. I turned the radio up full blast and put her hand on the dashboard. I could tell that she felt the vibrations and enjoyed the music. She began to laugh and jump to the music.

House
9 year old

Chapter Four

The Classroom

Designing a Place to Learn

When designing the physical layout of a classroom, take time to get to know your students before you begin making assumptions about their needs. After you have a grasp on learning styles, personal preferences, and personalities, design the layout of the classroom according to individual needs. Do not fix what is not broken.

If you are teaching in a self-contained classroom, visit several other classrooms, both regular and special education, for children of the same age. Make the classroom look like a classroom.

Have the classroom organized. Clutter is distracting for all children, but especially for children with autism, who have a need for order and sameness.

The classroom is a place for children to learn. Make it conducive to learning. Many times, well-meaning adults will disrupt a special education classroom when they would not think of disrupting a regular class. Remind outsiders that this is a class by running it like a class!

We expect children with disabilities to be included in regular classes, and yet we many times start them out in a room that is far removed from the regular class. Help your students by making the environments and what occurs in them as similar as possible. Look around and normalize.

The Color of Autism: **Neal**

I first met Neal when he was in kindergarten. He loved to read sight words from the Dolch word box and twiddle string. Neal could sing sound tracks from an entire Disney movie.

Neal pared life down to a few pleasures, and he enjoyed those with relish. He fought when the pleasures were denied him. Although a child of few words, and many of them taken from movies and commercials, he occasionally made statements that were so on target that he would leave people shaken. Neal never repeated himself, so you always hoped for a witness to reassure you that you had not imagined Neal's pearls of wisdom.

Neal was in the fourth grade when I visited him at his new home in another city. We had not been teacher and student for two years. We spent the day in his pool, splashing and laughing, without speaking more than ten words to each other.

Sharing good times with a person with autism is an acquired pleasure. You cannot force your idea of a good time on this person, no matter how hard you try. Once you get to the point where you can relax, respect one another's differences, and let things happen, each encounter is a memorable experience.

After swimming, Neal and I went to McDonald's for french fries. Neal liked to twiddle each fry before he ate it. I usually tried my student's little behaviors just to see if I could understand the fascination. So on this day, I also twiddled my fries. I found it somewhat comforting. We twiddled and ate, and ate and twiddled.

Although I usually keep the teacher's role in the classroom, it occasionally seeps over into social visits. I found myself becoming teacher as I asked Neal about his family in a style that we had become comfortable with when he had been in my class.

It went like this:

> Mommy is a _____. Neal filled in the blanks.
> Mommy is a <u>good mommy.</u>
> Daddy is a <u>good daddy.</u>
> Josh (my son) is a <u>good boy.</u>
> Neal is a <u>good boy.</u>

I was getting into the mesmerizing pattern of our talk and could have continued for some time. However, the next sequence jarred me out of the repetitious patter. I said, "Toni is". Neal twiddled a fry, looked me straight in the eye, and said, "the messenger."

Although I knew Neal would not repeat himself, I could not help but beg and plead for him to say it again just to make sure that I had heard him correctly. I offered more fries, more time in the pool, and new and better string to twiddle. But Neal picked up the last fry, twiddled it, and plopped it in his mouth. He ignored my pleas, stood up, took his trash to the proper place, and said, "Time to go." We left.

The Learning Environment

I hope that this book will help the student with autism learn in any classroom. The teacher will become "the messenger" and will attempt to bridge the gap between the person with autism's perception of the environment and the teacher's perception of an environment conducive to learning.

Becoming a partner in education with a person with autism is a challenging task. Without the partnership and the input of the person with autism, the journey will not be a productive one.

Some students with autism need very few changes in a traditional classroom. A minor tweak here and there can meet most of their needs. Assuming that all students with autism are going to need the same things is ridiculous. Get to know the student before you start knocking down walls or building towers.

Other students with autism will need many strategies to help them through their school day. However, without getting to know the student, you cannot predict what those strategies might be.

What works for one individual will not automatically fit another student's needs. Assuming that all students with autism need the same things will do all students with autism a disservice and will not adequately meet any student's needs.

Develop boundaries that are visually and physically defined

1. Boundaries are important to help the student "see," "feel," and "experience" where each area begins and ends.
2. Boundaries help to establish context. When an activity occurs in a predictable area each day, the student does not have to spend valuable time and energy trying to decide where to go. This eliminates the frustration that can build throughout the day while a student just tries to get to a destination.
3. Boundaries segment the classroom. Boundaries give the areas within the classroom meaning as to their purpose. Boundaries also give the student more tools to use in decoding the school environment. In our homes we do not have one room where everything occurs. We have rooms for different, clearly defined purposes. Remember this concept in arranging a classroom.

Create boundaries with existing materials

1. Use furniture to designate areas. Bookcases are especially helpful. They not only become physical boundaries, they also can store materials. Having relevant materials close at hand saves time for the teacher and increases the students' independence. This helps students identify objects with activities. Also, you are not locked into a permanent floor plan because you can move bookcases

if the occasion arises. Moving things around once or twice a year can help students with autism learn strategies for adjusting to changes in the environment.

You can cover bookcases with cloth to keep students from pulling out things. The cloth can also show what the particular area is. Find a cloth printed with pictures of books or letters for the reading area. Use a food motif for the snack area. If you are working with young children, use a print that pictures children at play for the play area. If you can find cloth with labeling words—so much the better.

Use solid color cloth and reinforce the teaching of colors or use cloth with shapes or numbers to reinforce these concepts. The possibilities are endless, so be creative. When you tire of one cloth, you can easily replace it with another. You can even make clothes to match the bookcase covers. Ok, so this is a little bit much, but I have known teachers to do such things.

Before attaching the cloth to the bookcases, hem the edges of the cloth so that it will not fray. Use either thumbtacks or staples to hold the cloth to the top of the bookcase. When you want to have access to the materials in the bookcase, lift the cloth and lay it on top of the bookcase.

2. You can use tape on the floor to define an area for a specific activity. Use different colors for different purposes. Tape for "lining up" can be blue, aerobics circle tape can be yellow, etc. Therefore, when you give directions such as, "Line up on the blue tape," or "go to the yellow circle," you are able to give more information. You can pair the verbal cue with a visual, such as a sign with a blue line, yellow circle, etc. Individual cue cards can convey the information to one student at a time.

Another suggestion for a defined "lining-up" area: Use large squares with numbers, letters, names, etc. fixed to the floor instead of a line. You can reinforce the number, letter, or name recognition (whichever you select) each time a student lines up. There are endless variations here, depending on the age and ability level of the student.

3. Carpets are good definition materials, especially for floor activities. Colors for different activities are an excellent way to define areas for different purposes.

    Carpets designed for children's playrooms can provide various themes. There are carpets with numbers, letters, designs, and pictures. There are play carpets with roads and towns printed on them.

    You can use carpet samples for individual seating. Their portability gives more options in forming groups, and you can remove them when you do not need them. Also, having a student get his or her own carpet, move it to where it needs to go, and put it away are all part of independence training.

The Color of Autism: **Mandy**

The carpet I inherited for my classroom caused much controversy among the other teachers and therapists. It was bright blue with a color wheel and basic shapes in the center. There was a bright yellow border of numbers and letters around the outside. The color and number words were printed in English and Spanish. People told me that the carpet had way too much information, was too bright, and would only distract the students with autism. However, individuals with autism do a beautiful job of making liars out of us. My students did not know that this carpet was bad for them. Mandy was one child who was fascinated by the carpet. She would crawl around its border during free time.

One day, little Mandy went to the cafeteria on her toes, as she was known to do. Her emerging language was delighting everyone. The lunch lady made Mandy request at least part of her lunch using words. Mandy and the lunch lady had developed a special relationship, and Mandy was appropriately using new words daily, especially when requesting her favorite foods.

However, no one was prepared for what happened one day. Mandy requested an apple, but the lunch lady did not hear her. Mandy did not scream as she had in the past when she did not get her way. She asked again, only this time, she gave more information. She said, "Red apple, please."

A lunchroom crisis was unfolding at the same time. The child in front of Mandy dropped his tray. He stepped in a mound of mashed potatoes. Milk oozed across the floor, and the lunch lady signaled for a mop. Other children chased peas and stomped them with gusto.

Mandy did not chase peas or giggle at the confusion. She was focused on the apple and how to get it. Mandy touched the lunch lady's arm and asked again, only this time she requested the apple using Spanish to define the color. The pea chase came to a halt as word spread that Mandy was not only using language to get her apple, she was also using a foreign language.

The lunch lady was so excited that she gave Mandy one apple, then another, and then another. With three apples on her tray, Mandy studied them and announced, "Three apples" and tiptoed to her place at the table.

Labeling within Boundaries Helps Give Meaning to the Defined Area

1. Walls are wonderful backgrounds for information. Daily, weekly, and individual class schedules can all have a place on the wall.

2. Use walls to designate different instructional areas like the music area, calendar area, circle area, computer space, reading area, and learning centers.

3. Using walls to label different areas is good practice for when students are in the community. We all have to know how to search for restrooms, find different sections of stores, or find items within sections of stores.

4. Labeling chairs with students' names is good practice for younger students. Chairs and their use can be fitted to the individual student, thus the beginning of awareness of name and property. Some individuals need a chair for each specific purpose; others are comfortable moving their chairs from one activity to another. Moving chairs is good for gross motor development and a sense of accomplishment. Many times, too much is done for children with autism or other disabilities. The very act of doing for oneself, whether it is done correctly or not, is a vital part of the learning experience.

- *We learn when we try.*

- *We learn when we fail.*

- *We learn when we are given the opportunity to try again.*

- *We do not learn when a task is done for us.*

- *We learn dependency and helplessness when others continually do a task for us.*

- *When we learn to do a task ourselves, we learn to take one more step alone.*

Possible Areas to Consider When Setting Up Boundaries

1. Free-time area

This can be an area to play or indulge in a little relaxation. Relaxation for students with autism might consist of twiddling a string, running small wheels over their faces, looking through colored glass, or any number of self-stimulatory activities.

2. Quiet-time area

Soothing areas with a rocking chair, beanbag, or place to lie down can calm a person. You may need to set this area apart from the rest of the room with dividers. This will give the person a sense of privacy.

Have favorite calming activities available in this area: music, bits of string, flipping items, hand-held computer games, etc.

Having an area to go to can decrease behaviors. Instead of using "time out" when behaviors escalate, teach the person to go to the quiet area to help manage stress before it builds to an explosion.

3. Group area

Develop as many group areas as needed. The students' needs will define the necessary number.

A large table could be one of the group areas. If you used a different table for each activity, you would run out of floor space. Give the table multiple uses with a sign, using both pictures and words that can be changed when the activity changes. For example, when it is snack time, the sign could have food pictures with the word "snack" under the pictures. For crafts, use a picture of glue, paste, scissors, and paints with the word "crafts" under it.

4. Circle area

An area you designate as a circle area can encompass many activities. Use it for music activities, socialization, stories, and much, much more. Using the circle time each day at a certain time for a certain activity gives it definition.

5. Work area

Each student needs a space to call his or her own for work time. This space can be a desk or table. A desk provides its own boundaries. If table space is shared, a piece of tape down the middle may be enough of a boundary for some students. If the student needs a more concrete boundary, a carrel clearly defines the individual workspace. Some students may need even more privacy in order to concentrate. A walled-off area minimizes visual distractions.

Once again, start with the norm for a regular class and add modifications as needed. Do not limit students by assuming they are going to need this or that. Assume that they can do what everyone else is doing and go from there.

6. Transition area

This is the area that you might use the most. The student learns to come to the transition area when an activity ends. This signals the end of one activity and the beginning of another. However, if the student easily moves from one activity to the next, you can eliminate the transition area. Individualize!

Self Portrait
6 year old

Chapter Five

Schedules

Making Sense of the School Day

How many of you rely on your daily planner to get you through the day, week, and year without missing appointments? Individuals with autism also need a system to guide them through the day. Here are points to consider when developing a schedule for them:

• Tailor the schedule to the individual

• Give the student control over his or her schedule

• Be consistent in the use of the schedule

• Allow for flexibility when designing a schedule

• Solicit input from the student when designing the schedule

• Designate a signal for using the schedule and be consistent. For example, say, "Check your schedule," set a timer, etc.

• Use the daily, or weekly schedule to fill your individual schedules (See "Activities")

There are many different ways to develop a schedule. The following is an outline:

1. Object Schedule
2. Transition to Photograph Schedule
3. Partial or Full-Day Photograph – strip or folder
4. Transition to Partial or Full-Day Line Drawing/Identifying Word Card – strip or folder

5. Partial or Full-Day Line Drawing/Identifying Word Card – strip or folder
6. Transition to Word Schedule
7. Partial or Full-Day Word Schedule – strip or folder

At each level of planning, the student can learn to fill in his or her own schedule. This gives people more control over their day and life. It also works to reduce the cue dependency that so many children with autism develop. (See *The Fine Art of Cueing.*)

Filling one's schedule should be sequencing with a purpose. Filling out the daily schedule should be a structured activity and done at a set time. There are times when it is not practical for the student to complete his or her own schedule, and staff members need to determine when the time is right. You should probably wait until the student is at the photograph schedule level to begin working on filling the schedule.

There are many different ways to develop a schedule. The following are only examples:

1. Object Schedule
Design: Use the actual object to show the student what to do. For example, use a cup to designate the time to eat, a pencil for work time, a ball for gym class, etc.

Control: Designate a place for the schedule. The student goes to the schedule, picks up the object, and takes it to the place where the activity will occur. Designate a place at the activity site for the student to place the object before beginning the activity.

2. **Transition to Photograph Schedule** Place a photograph of the person doing the activity in the designated area that has been used for the object schedule. Have the corresponding picture on an envelope in the activity area. Show the student how to place the picture in the envelope. As the student masters the skill, replace the object schedule with the photograph strip schedule (see *Donald*).

3. Partial or Full-Day Photograph Strip Schedule

Design: Identify the activities for the day, either for a partial day (partial photograph schedule) or full day (full-day photograph schedule). Following the weekly class schedule (see Chapter Nine), the activities for a partial day for Monday could be:

Book bag (a.m.)
Aerobics
Circle I Greetings
Calendar
Music
Lunch

Following the weekly class schedule (see Chapter Nine), the activities for a full day on Monday could be:

Book bag (a.m.)
Aerobics
Circle I Greetings
Calendar
Music
Lunch
Break or Recess
Circle II Cassette
Academics
Reading I, II or III
Snack/Dishes
Arts/Crafts
Book
Book bag (p.m.)
Dismissal

Take two pictures of the student doing each activity. Make a strip using poster board. Use right-to-left or top-to-bottom order. You can use Velcro® instead of the paper clip method; however, Velcro® can be expensive and difficult to maintain. Go for the easiest method for all to use. Attach the strip to the wall and mark the student's name on it.

Cut the top off an envelope and attach the envelope to the wall in the area where the activity will take place. Put one of the photographs on the outside of the envelope. The other photograph goes in the appropriate place on the schedule.

Control: When you give the cue to check the schedule, the student goes to the board, removes the first picture, and takes it to the site of the activity. The student matches the pictures and places the photograph inside the envelope. This works well for activities that take place in the same classroom.

When the student leaves the classroom and goes to another, simply have an envelope outside the classroom for the student to slip the picture in it before he or she enters the room. Other students in the school quickly learn to respect this method and will protect the envelopes. As students remove pictures from their schedules, they can see how many activities remain.

At lunchtime, use a picture of the students eating lunch in their usual places. The student carries the picture to the cafeteria and hands it to the cashier in return for a lunch. The cashier can then put the picture back in the teacher's mailbox for use the next day.

When the schedule is empty, the student or staff replenishes it for the next portion of the day, or if a full-day is being used, for the next day.

4. Partial or Full-Day Folder Photograph Schedule

Design: Use a folder instead of a strip. This helps students who travel from room to room. Make pockets for the photographs to slip in and out of. Make the pockets large enough to keep the photographs in place, but not so large that they obscure the photo. Velcro® is an alternative. Have the photographs in top-to-bottom or left-to-right order. The photograph folder schedule can become a little heavy when doing a full-day, so you can reduce the photographs on a copy machine. This not only reduces the size, but it can also reduce the weight. You can add needed additional pages to the folder.

Control: Use the same procedure you used for the photograph strip schedule.

5. Transition to Partial or Full-Day Line Drawing/ Identifying Word Card—strip or folder

If the students have mastered a full-day folder photograph schedule and are using it to go from class to class, they are probably ready for the line drawing/identifying word card strip or folder.

6. Partial or Full-Day Line Drawing/Identifying Word Card Strip Schedule

Design:
The student may begin at this level or progress to it through the Object Photograph Schedules. You can use the same strip that you used for the Photograph Schedule for the Line Drawing/ Identifying Word Card Schedule. Mayer-Johnson has an extensive collection of line drawings with the identifying word underneath each.[1]

Laminate the cards to add to their life span. Every week a few of the cards would make it home in my pockets and go through the washer and dryer. This is another reason Velcro® is not as practical. Velcro® will come off the card in the washer or dryer and end up attached to a silk blouse.

Control: The student checks the schedule when given the cue to do so. He or she removes the line drawing/identifying word card and takes it to the site of the activity. Use the same envelope method (or one of your own design) as detailed in the Photograph Schedule section. However, instead of using photographs on the outside of the envelope, use the identical line drawing/ identifying word card. The student matches the line drawing/ identifying word card to the one that is attached to the outside of the envelope.

1. Mayer-Johnsonis a publishing company offering excellent educational materials(www.mayerjohnson.com)

Using the line drawing/identifying word cards throughout the day will have the additional benefit of teaching students sight words that are relevant to their day. The identifying words can then be reinforced as spelling words during the student's individual academic work time. The student has a visual for how many activities are left in the morning or in the entire day.

7. Line Drawing/Identifying Word Folder Schedule

Use a folder with pockets or Velcro® to hold the line drawing/identifying word cards in a top-to-bottom or left-to-right manner. The student removes the line drawing/identifying word card and places it in the designated place.

When students reach this level, it is possible that they will be doing more seat work than going to activity sites. If so, the student can have a folder for each designated seat work activity with the identifying line drawing/identifying word card on the outside of an envelope. The student removes the card from his folder, places it in the envelope on the outside of the work folder, opens the folder, and completes the task. The student or a staff member then refills the schedule when it is empty.

8. Transition to Word Schedule

When the student shows an understanding of the word portion of the Line Drawing/Identifying Word Card, begin transitioning the student to the Word Schedule. Word schedules are a more sophisticated way to keep track of the day and are best used in folder, notebook, or calendar form. However, do not discount the idea of using a strip schedule if that is what works best with the student.

Transition by slowly replacing the Line Drawing/Identifying Word Card with a few word cards. If the student has paper and pencil skills, he can create a word schedule.

9. Full-Day Word Schedule (for students without paper and pencil skills)

Design: Create a laminated sheet with the blocks of time down the left side and leave a space beside each block to attach Velcro®. If the schedule varies from day to day, use a sheet for each day of the week.

The student has an envelope with word cards needed for each activity of the day. Each word card has Velcro® attached to the back so that it can be placed on the Velcro® that is by the correct block of time.

Control: The student creates his or her schedule by following a master sheet or a posted schedule of the day's activities. When the student completes an activity, the student removes the word card and places it back in the envelope.

Note: There can be many steps between the Full-Day Word Schedule for students without paper and pencil skills and the Full-Day Word Schedule for students with such skills. Adapt the planner to the students' needs. Whatever works is the best method for any individual student.

10. Full-Day Word Schedule (for students with paper and pencil skills)

Design:
Copy a single piece of paper with the blocks of time corresponding to the day's schedule for the student to use. If the schedule varies from day to day, the student could have a printed page for every day of the week. This idea is similar to the daily planners that many of us use to keep track of our appointments. Place the pages in a folder for the student to carry with him or her during the school day.

Control: The student fills in his schedule either for the day or for the entire week. When an activity is complete, he can check it off. Some students may need a box beside the activity to give more structure to the process. They can check the box when they finish the activity.

Creative Schedules—Made for Individual Students

1. Shoe Box Schedule

One of my students loved his schedule, but he also loved to drop things from any height and watch as they disappeared. The window was a favorite drop point. We took his half-day, line drawing/identifying word schedule and put it on top of a shoe box. We cut a slit at the end of the top of the shoe box and when he pulled his activity off, he could drop it in the slot and watch it disappear. His throwing things out the window decreased dramatically. Over the years, I have used the shoe box schedule for many different students and in many different settings.

If the student wants to see the cards as they go into the slot, you can use a clear plastic shoe box, found at any store that sells closet organizers. The box itself, whether clear or not, becomes an excellent place to store the cards.

2. Necklace Schedule

When students travel from one class to another, you have to be creative to help them take their schedule with them in a way that is easy to keep track of.

One such schedule for younger students is a simple necklace schedule. A small strip of heavy paper is laminated and the needed schedule is attached with Velcro®.

Put the necklace around the child's neck with a chain or piece of yarn. For example, a student is going to music class and needs to have a schedule for what to do in that class. The necklace we used had three pictures on it.

They were sit down (on the chair labeled with their name), sing, and play instrument.

3. Locker Schedule

For older students, the locker can be a jungle all unto itself. The daily schedule can be taped inside the locker door to be another visual reminder of what to do and where to go.

4. Magnetic Schedule

You can purchase magnetic paper wherever creative computer paper is sold, and create schedules with your computer. These schedules can be used on a cookie sheet, piece of sheet metal, magnetic chalkboard, refrigerator, file cabinet, ironing board, metal chair, etc.

5. Book Bag Schedule

Attach a schedule to the book bag to help the student keep his or her day organized. I found a clear book bag that does wonders for visual organization. The schedule could be put inside the clear pocket, and all of the things in the book bag are visible.

6. Stick-On Schedule

You can purchase window decal sheets wherever creative computer paper is sold, and create schedules with your computer. Put them on mirrors, glass, refrigerators, file cabinets, computer screens, etc.

7. Book Schedule

A schedule can be in book form and carried around with the student. There are many ways to do this. Each page could be a different class or activity within the school. There might be another book for activities at home and in the community.

8. Cork Board Schedule

You can purchase cork in rolls or different size squares. Some students enjoy the fine motor skill of attaching a schedule to the cork with thumbtacks. There are also many different types of thumbtacks.

The Color of Autism: Donald

Donald rapidly learned to use his schedule (full-day/line drawing/ identifying word strip). Then he rapidly learned to manipulate it for his own purposes.

The classroom chalkboard displayed the schedule. Donald's schedule was made of a strip of tag board with slits cut out along the bottom. The slit was big enough for a paper clip to fit through it. The activity cards were slipped onto the paper clip and could be easily removed and replaced.

Donald loved community outings. Since the bus symbol represented an outing, he coveted this particular card. He would get on the eraser ledge of the chalkboard and reach for the envelopes that were above each schedule strip. The envelopes held all the activity cards that were needed for each person's schedule.

Donald would precariously balance there while he removed the bus card from his envelope, move slowly down the chalk ledge, and remove the bus card from everyone else's storage envelope. Then he would quickly replace all of his activity cards with bus cards. This could be done in just a few minutes and always when Donald saw that all of the adults in the classroom were busy elsewhere. When one of us discovered Donald's altered schedule, we guided Donald through the process of returning his schedule to reality, and his schedule once again reflected the true day.

This could annoy the person who had to help Donald repair his schedule, but it gave us a valuable glimpse into Donald's wants and desires. It also showed us how aware Donald was of our every move. It took Donald a few months to realize that placing the bus card on the schedule did not make a community trip happen. When he became aware of the regular occurrence of our community outings, he stopped trying to conjure them up.

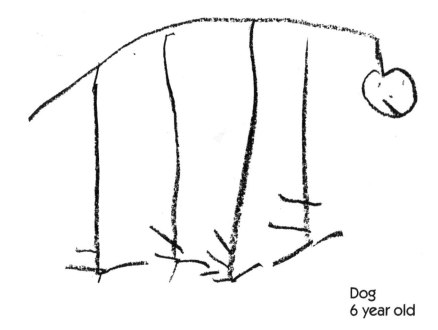

Dog
6 year old

Chapter Six

The Fine Art of Cueing

It is important to step back and take a look at how you are cueing individuals. Many times we are working so hard to teach a skill that we do not realize that we are making the student "cue-dependent" when we should be striving for independence.

Each of us learns by having the opportunity to make mistakes and then try again. Individuals with autism learn in the same way.

The following is the hierarchy of cues:

1) Wait and See

The first cue should always be no cue. Step back and take a "wait and see" approach. It is a valuable, ongoing tool for evaluation, both of self and the student.

Give the student a chance to respond. Remember that everyone has individual learning styles, and many people with autism have delays in processing information. Many often appear to learn a skill overnight. Like most seemingly overnight successes, however, a tremendous amount of behind-the-scenes work has gone into the eventual success. Give people the opportunity to demonstrate their capabilities (and they can change daily) before jumping in with assistance.

2) Verbal Cue

Start with a cue that will direct the person to the tool that will help him achieve his independence. For example, when teaching the person to use a schedule, cue the person by saying, "Check your schedule."

3) Model Activity for the Student

Some activities are easier and more appropriate to model than others. Do not turn your teaching style into a game of charades. Sometimes it is more effective to use peers to model activities.

4) Review Steps Needed to Complete Activity

Review at the student's level. Use his or her learning style to direct your review. Always remind yourself to do less than you are inclined to do.

5) Physical Assistance

Physical assistance can be a light touch, or you can take the person to the activity and guide him or her through it. Use physical assistance as a last resort and conduct assistance with respect for the individual. Do not automatically use physical assistance. Give the person the opportunity to try the activity on his or her own.

6) Review and Refine

The perfect time to review what is successful and what needs to be redone is when the person is actually going through the process of attempting a task. Make mental notes and rework the system before attempting the next time.

Videotaping is an excellent way to review a student's progress. It also gives insight into the methods used by the teacher, the give and take between teacher and student, and how the student is responding to the lesson.

An Example of Cueing

James comes into the classroom with his winter coat, hat, mittens, and book bag.

Cue: Wait and see

James drops the book bag at the door and runs to the play area with hat, coat, and mittens still on.

Cue: Verbal reminder to check schedule

James uses a Partial-Day Photograph Schedule, and the first photograph card is a photo of him hanging his supplies on the hook under his name. James gets a puzzle and dumps it on the floor.

Cue: Review steps needed to complete activity

The teacher takes James to his wall schedule and points to the first photograph card. The teacher gives James a verbal cue: "Hang up coat and book bag." James pulls away from the teacher.

Cue: Review steps needed to complete activity

The teacher brings James back to the schedule and hands him the first card of a photograph of himself putting his things away.

Cue: Wait and see

James goes to the closet and places the card in an envelope attached at his eye level. On the outside of the envelope is a similar photograph of himself putting his things away. (The photograph is almost identical since it was taken at the same time as the other photo). James stands by the coat hook. He does not take off his coat.

Cue: Review steps needed to complete activity

The teacher points to a picture sequence strip that is attached to the wall next to James' hook. James' name is on a card above the hook. The print in his name is consistent with all other postings around the classroom and on the work and homework folders. The teacher points to each step on the sequence strip while giving James verbal cues. She takes James' finger and points to each step. "Take off coat. Hang up coat." James takes his coat off and drops it to the floor.

Cue: Physical assistance

The teacher assists James with picking up his coat using hand over hand. Together they hang the coat on the hook. The teacher praises James for doing the job.

Review and refine

The teacher realizes that she needs to break down the tasks. She takes new photographs of James hanging up only the book bag, returning to the schedule, getting a photograph of hanging up his coat, and then returning to the planner to get a photograph of putting away his hat, and so forth.

The teacher reviews all other parts of the day to determine their clarity and if she should break any other activity into smaller tasks.

Chapter Seven

To Self-Stim or Not to Self-Stim

Two rules to consider for self-stimulation:

1. If the self-stimulation does not interfere with the person's learning process, **leave it alone!** Let the person engage in something that obviously feels good. How many of us would rebel if we were not allowed to wiggle our feet or play with our ink pen during long meetings? The key is being able to stop the self-stim when it is time to learn and work. You cannot work on the computer if your hands are engaged in twiddling or spinning an object.

2. If the self-stimulation is not interfering with another person's learning process or personal space, **leave it alone!** When you try to interfere with a self-stimulatory activity, and sometimes you must, have the person with autism and everyone else take part in selecting a replacement. Sometimes your goal is to find a more socially acceptable replacement, other times the goal is to ensure the safety of the person with autism, and sometimes it is for the safety of others.

If you try to make the person go "cold turkey" without his stim, or replace it with something totally off-base, the person will usually find his own replacement that can be as obtrusive, or even more so, than the original stim.

Do not get so focused on the self-stimulation that you create something more bizarre. Use common sense and start with the most obvious approach. Be consistent among all environments. The story of Bill is one example of how consistency is important.

The Color of Autism: **Bill**

I had not seen Bill for at least two years when I got a phone call from his current teacher requesting help. Bill had started holding water in his mouth, and this was driving everyone crazy.

The teacher had developed a behavior plan that went like this: When Bill held water in his mouth, the teacher told him to go to the bathroom. The teacher or assistant would accompany him to the bathroom and request that he spit the water into the sink. He usually complied.

At home, Bill's mother would hold his nose and rub his neck until he swallowed. He seemed to thoroughly enjoy all the attention that his holding water was bringing his way.

As I observed the class one day, Bill signed, "Drink." The teacher let him go into the hallway to get a drink of water. Bill came back to class with his cheeks puffed out and water dripping down his chin. The teacher looked at me and gestured helplessly. I took a deep breath, walked over to Bill, looked him in the eye, and said, "Swallow." He did, and this was the beginning of the end of the problem.

Several things probably happened. First, the teachers and parent had focused on the water, thus creating a problem. As they tried more and more solutions, the importance of the water holding grew for Bill. It became a way for him to get attention, and it was a fun game. Bill did not give up the behavior the day I was present, but telling him to swallow worked in all environments, and he eventually gave up holding water.

Granted, my simplistic solution could have failed; however, the point is to begin with a common-sense approach and go from there. Do not start with a complicated four- or five-page plan and then wonder why the whole thing has gotten out of hand.

Guessing the Reasons for the Behavior

Trying to second-guess behaviors is a tricky job. If you do stumble upon the reason for a behavior, it certainly does help to work through it. You can assist the person with autism in finding a more acceptable way of expressing his needs.

Many times, however, it is an endless guessing game, and one that you will probably lose. This does not mean that you should give up. It just means that many times your frame of reference and the person with autism's frame of reference are light years apart. When you begin understanding the individual and respecting his way of thinking, the guessing game gets easier. You need to learn to read the clues that many times elude us because the perceptions of people without autism can be so different from those of people with autism. The job is challenging and can be exciting. It is always refreshing to see things from a new angle, and people with autism can certainly give a new twist to your view of the world.

The Color of Autism: **Roger**

Roger accepted new clothes and seemed to enjoy them. Yet once a shirt had been washed, he began picking at the sleeves. He would look at the sleeve and pluck at it over and over until small holes formed. The plucking made bigger and bigger holes until it ruined the shirt.

Many strategies did not work. Short-sleeved shirts, striped shirts, checked shirts, and solid-colored shirts were all victims. Bright-colored shirts and muted-colored shirts also did not escape from the plucking. Only white shirts worked. In the trials and errors of the shirt-shredding mystery, Roger's mother discovered that light-colored, short-sleeved shirts lasted longer. Soon, Roger's wardrobe consisted of all light-colored, short-sleeved shirts. This did not stop the destruction; it only gave each shirt a slightly longer life.

Years later, Roger began communicating through facilitated communication. When his mother asked why he tore his shirts, Roger replied that it was because once he detected lint on a shirt, usually after it had been washed, he thought the lint was dirt. He could not stand to wear a "dirty'" shirt. Roger was trying to remove the dirt and make the shirt clean again. As he plucked at the miniscule pieces of lint, his fingers would leave behind more traces of lint. The plucking soon left a hole. The hole would have tiny strands of fabric that Roger had to remove, producing a larger hole.

Why did Roger tear up dark shirts faster than light-colored shirts? You probably have enough information by now to answer this one. You cannot see lint as easily on a light-colored shirt. However, if you look close enough, you can see it.

After years of second-guessing why Roger tore up his shirts, not one person correctly guessed Roger's reason. He did not shred the shirts to be destructive, which was almost everyone's first guess.

Roger did not tear them up because he did not want to wear them. He did not rip at them out of frustration over random daily events he did not like and could not control. He did not tear up his shirts because he did not like the color or style. All of Roger's years of shirt destruction were not an effort to destroy his shirts but an attempt to keep them new and perfect.

Replace Some Behaviors with Less Noticeable Ones

Here are some self-stimulations that may warrant replacement:
- Sniffing people's hair
- Being aggressive toward self and/or others
- Twirling strings attached to someone's clothing
- Twirling strings
- Twiddling objects like strings, pencils, straws, sticks, etc.
- Making loud noises

- Holding onto something at all times (could be small object or toy)
- Spinning one's self
- Running
- Screaming

Always consider the situation, the environment, and the person with autism before making the decision to replace, limit, or eliminate a self-stimulatory activity.

Some possible replacements (consider these as a starting point only):

- Sniffing people's hair could be the smell of the shampoo or conditioner that is drawing the person to a certain head. Suggest that the "sniffee" change her/his hair products. If the "sniffor" persists, saturate a small piece of cotton with the hair product for the person with autism to carry in his or her pocket and sniff discretely.

- Twirling strings attached to someone else's clothing is self-stimming. Start with a string of his or her own clothing (now you run the risk of creating a new self-stim).

- Twirling strings and twiddling objects like strings, pencils, straws, sticks, etc. There probably is not a substitute for a good twiddle or twirl, so limiting the time spent on these activities is a good place to start. Use the stim as a reward for the time the child spends on task.

- Making loud noises. Build in time for noise, such as loud play at recess. Revel in loud noises at these times. The louder the better. Celebrate noise and create new noises. Use instruments to make loud noises and call it music.

- Holding onto something at all times. Try having the child leave the "something" (object) at home. Of course, the child will fuss and perhaps throw a tantrum, but give the method some time to work before you consider another plan of action. Or, you can remove the object when the person is doing a favorite activity and increase the time without the object. Making the environment as meaningful as possible will help with all aspects of the day for the child (and for you, too).

- Spinning one's body. The answer to many self-stims is to engage the person in a meaningful activity that requires him or her to stop the stim. However, one of the problems with this is that the self-stim is probably the most meaningful activity for the person with autism. As the environment begins to make sense, it becomes easier and easier to redirect his or her activities.

- Running. Do not focus on the running. Remember to focus on learning new skills instead of losing a behavior. If you do not make running a game, it loses its allure. Of course, if a person is in danger, you chase him!

- Screaming. This is one of the hardest behaviors of all to replace. The screamer has total control over his or her vocal chords. Once again, make the environment meaningful. This can take time, and screaming can quickly get on people's nerves.

  Try taping the screaming and play the tape back to the screamer. You could also videotape the person screaming. Video can be effective because it allows the person to experience how his or her behavior affects others.

  Peers can leave the screamer alone to scream. Ignoring the screamer will weed out those who are screaming to get attention.

  Whatever avenue you choose, screaming is a difficult behavior to control.

The Color of Autism: **Trina, Molly, and Annie**

Trina was a screamer. She screamed when she was angry. She screamed when she was happy. She screamed for the sheer joy of it. Her screams were loud and piercing. When Trina was busy, she did not scream; keeping her busy, however, was not an easy task. There were not many things that interested Trina other than screaming. If it were something she did not want to do, she would scream in protest. Looking back, I realize she received a great deal of attention from screaming.

Since there were several girls in the program for children with autism, I decided that they should experience a slumber party. Molly, Annie, and Trina accepted my invitation.

Molly was a charmer who would tell nursery rhymes and include you as one of the characters. She also banged her head against any object she could find. The brick walls at school were her favorite place to bang. She wore a helmet much of the time.

Annie liked to inspect your clothes and ask if the items were new. She preferred to take her own clothes off every chance she got and put them back on, inside out. Annie didn't care where she disrobed, and this caused many embarrassing situations.

And, of course, Trina screamed.

Julie, the program's speech therapist, agreed to help me with the slumber party. We had a fairly uneventful dinner. We got everyone into pajamas and were feeling quite pleased with our little venture.

When the lights went out, Trina began screaming, and Molly began banging her head on the wall. It was a rhythmic thump, thump, thump. We turned on the lights, thinking the darkness had triggered all the self-stimulating activity. The screaming persisted, however, and the thumping got stronger. We sang to Trina and reasoned with Molly, but to no avail. Thump, thump, thump. Scream, scream, scream.

Someone pounded on the door. When we opened it, there stood the apartment manager and two policemen. They peered around me into the room. Annie had removed her pajamas and was in the process of trying to put them on inside out.

I tried to explain the situation, but this was pre-*Rain Man*. Those were the days when a substitute teacher came to school with a large bag of art supplies because she had been told she was substituting at the artistic center.

I told the police that we were having a slumber party with our students who had autism. The looks on their faces told me that they did not comprehend why the children were acting so bizarre and out of control. At first, they expressed concern that we were in danger, but as they looked at the three little girls, I was sure they thought we were torturing the children. I quickly dropped the word autism, realizing that this was not the time or place to educate anyone. I explained that the children were our special education students, and we were simply having a slumber party. I even offered to let the police use my phone to call the children's parents for verification. It was not until I asked for suggestions to quiet Trina and keep Molly still that they declined to help and left with warnings of, "Quiet down, or else."

Julie and I quickly brainstormed. We kept Molly from pounding by feeding her mass quantities of popcorn, one kernel at a time. Annie stayed quiet as long as we left her pajamas on inside out.

Trina responded to nothing. We turned on music to help mask her screams, and she finally screamed herself to sleep.

Looking back on this episode, I realize how far we have come with autism awareness. I rarely mention autism when someone in the group has not heard of, or been personally affected by, this syndrome.

If I could do the slumber party again, I would not bring the children to a strange environment and expect them to appreciate my desire for them to experience a slumber party. I would not do away with the idea entirely, but I probably would not be as ambitious. I might start smaller and just do dinner the first time. I could build up to an overnight. I would spend time preparing the children for this event with stories and pictures and maybe a mini-trial run. I would use the stories and pictures to discuss expectations. Also, once the slumber party started, I would not put Molly on an open-back couch with a wall at her disposal.

Knowing what we know today about sensory issues and autism, I would have realized that Annie was probably reacting to the roughness of the clothes against her body. She found them softer and more tolerable inside out.

Trina is still a mystery, however. I have only encountered one other such determined screamer, but that is another story. We probably spent too much time trying to keep Trina from screaming and not enough time trying to engage her in things that would have helped her make sense of her environment. I'm sure we were a big part of her screaming and not a part of any solution.

I cannot say whether the girls enjoyed the evening. Hopefully, they took something away from it. It certainly was an experience that I will never forget. I developed a fresh perspective for what it must be like for the families that lived with these challenging young ladies. I gained a healthy respect for all involved.

The Color of Autism: **Ken**

Ken loved to spin round and round. The teachers always said, "No spinning." Usually they had to stop him physically and sit him down. The minute he was up, off he would go spinning. The school director had recently returned from a workshop on autism and was full of new ideas. "Let him spin," she announced. "He will tire of it, and we will be done with it."

One day Ken came in, dropped his coat and book bag, and began spinning. He had recently added a hop to his spin. His shiny black hair bounced and twirled with each revolution. Ken continued to spin for most of the morning. His face became red and coated with a film of sweat.

One of the teachers disappeared at lunchtime. She came back waving a special education journal. "Look at this," she shouted. There was an article on children with autism that denounced the "let them spin" philosophy. The spinning would only feed the need to spin, and the child would possibly never stop. Panic ensued as professionals descended on Ken, pulling him out of his frenzied hop and spin.

Focus on Learning a Skill Instead of Changing a Behavior

The answer to many self-stims is to engage the person in a meaningful activity. One of the problems is that the self-stim is the most meaningful activity to the person at the time. However, as the environment begins to make sense to the person with autism, redirection of self-stimming becomes easier and easier.

In my early days of working with individuals with autism, I spent days trying to eliminate one behavior or another. We teachers spent time discussing various methods for different children. Most of the individual plans we wrote focused on these behaviors.

Today, a more proactive approach eliminates some behaviors. Instead of focusing on the behavior, focus on the essential skills.

When the spotlight is on learning a skill instead of losing a behavior, changes begin to take place. As the world around a person with autism takes on significance, the need for some self-stimulatory behavior decreases. My work with J.J. demonstrates this.

The Color of Autism: J.J.

J.J. was a runner. He had a colorful reputation when he entered kindergarten. His parents were terrified that he would bolt from the school, never to be seen again. J.J.'s doors at home had sophisticated lock systems, yet he ran blocks from his house in the middle of the night. He slipped away from babysitters, relatives, and day care workers. J.J. was a master runner.

In the first few weeks of school, J.J. ran from the classroom over and over again. He was always chased by the youngest of the staff. She wore her best running shoes daily. She never spoke to J.J. when she caught him, but she always brought him back to the activity he had been engaged in before he ran. Soon, she stopped chasing him. She kept him in sight and demanded that he return to class.

J.J.'s education plan included all the skills learned in a regular kindergarten, with adaptations to his learning style. He did a packet of work each day. Much of the work was repetitive and designed to go from hand over hand to minimal assistance from an adult. J.J. practiced printing his name, address, and phone number. At first he traced raised letters with his finger. He then started tracing over dotted letters with a pencil. He progressed to forming letters on his own. J.J. worked on kindergarten math as well.

J.J. spent the rest of the day doing short activities with peer tutors at his side. He spent an hour each day in a regular kindergarten class.

At the end of the first six weeks, J.J. no longer ran from the class. If anything, he ran **to** class. The classroom had meaning. We had not emphasized the running or allowed it to become a game. We expected J.J. to remain in class, and he did.

Given the opportunity, many students will not only show you how to help them change a task to better suit them, but in some instances they will discover strategies on their own.

The Color of Autism: **Arron**

About three weeks into a new school year, Arron started to cover his ears when the xylophone sounded for the end-of-the-day announcements. He then began covering his ears in anticipation of the xylophone.

Soon Arron covered his ears after lunch, even though the time for the xylophone was three hours away. Arron's anxiety over the impending noise prevented him from learning in the afternoon.

The students in Arron's fifth grade class decided to try to solve the problem so that Arron would not waste the entire afternoon waiting for the dreaded xylophone. Some of their suggestions were:

- Do away with the xylophone and begin the announcements without the xylophone and just start talking.

- Do not broadcast the announcements. Send a memo around at the end of the day to be read to the students.

- Have Arron leave the building before the xylophone sounds.

- Turn the volume down.

- Have Arron wear headphones and listen to his favorite music while the xylophone and announcements sounded.

These were all creative, valid suggestions; however, none of them would help Arron stop covering his ears. The class eventually decided to help Arron instead of enabling him.

The students suggested that Arron be present in the office while the xylophone was being played. The students felt that if Arron saw the xylophone, his anxiety might decrease.

Arron and a peer went to the office daily for a week. Arron did not resist the visits, but he still covered his ears. The class was about to give up on this strategy and try another when Arron took matters into his own hands, literally.

Every day, Arron moved closer to the xylophone. On the sixth day, he removed one hand from one ear. He attempted to cover the ear by tilting his head and bringing his shoulder up to meet it. The other hand was still firmly clasped over the other ear.

Arron reached out with his free hand and took the stick away from the xylophone player. He played the three-note ditty and smiled. The next day he arrived in class and requested, "Play xylophone, please." Everyone agreed that this was a very good idea.

Arron still covered his ears for other reasons, but one obstacle to learning had been conquered; and as a result, Arron's afternoons were productive once again.

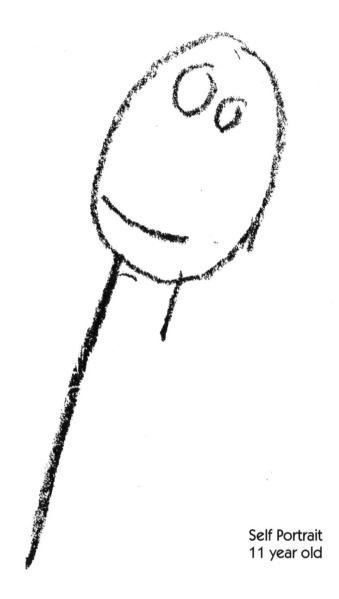

Self Portrait
11 year old

Chapter Eight

School and Beyond

Homework

Why Homework Is Essential for Students in the Autism Spectrum

- Homework helps the student reinforce a skill.

- Homework can give the student the opportunity to transfer one earning from one environment to another.

- Homework can become a bridge between home and school.

- Homework can give the family the opportunity to see the student in another light.

- Homework gives the school and family common ground when discussing the student.

- Homework can increase the student's self-esteem. Siblings see their brother or sister with autism doing the same thing they are doing.

- Homework helps the family learn new ways to teach the student.

- Homework can transfer to other household activities.

When I first began giving homework to my students with autism, I had this clear image of myself sitting at the kitchen table after the dinner dishes had been cleared away. I'd get out my books, paper, and favorite pens and pencils.

When you work with students with autism, you have to rethink many things. You want to keep the basic structure, but you have to make it meaningful for the student.

Homework for a student with autism may be paper and pencil activities; but then again it may have nothing to do with paper and pencil. It all depends on the students and their needs at the time.

The Color of Autism: **Dominick**

Everyone in my class had homework four nights a week. I always gave them Friday off. It was sometimes difficult to find homework for students when we struggled to find meaningful activities that would fill their school day.

Dominick was one of those students for whom we struggled to find meaningful homework. What we discovered may surprise you.

I always tried to make my students as independent as possible. I realized very early that there was a detrimental side to "doing for" a student. All the student learns is dependency not independence.

Lunchtime was a challenge for my students with autism because our school served french fries several times a week, and most of my students would not touch a french fry without ketchup. The ketchup was in those little packets that can be maddening to open.

Dominick loved ketchup, but he could not open those little packets. Although the lunchroom or the fast food restaurant was the natural place to teach this skill, Dominick was so focused on his fries that we could not get him to focus on opening the packet without help.

Dominick's homework became five packets of ketchup a night. I wrote the following plan for opening his packets:

> Dominick will use a pincer grasp with both hands on top of the packet. He will use a twisting motion to tear the packet open. Do not let him use his teeth. Assist him in getting his hands and fingers in the right position and let him do it independently. Encourage him to "use pressure," "focus," and "try again." Use hand over hand, if needed, to show him how it feels to apply the right amount of pressure to the packet.

It was a happy day when Dominick's envelope came back with five flat, empty packets in it. I still have one of those little empty packets in my desk.

Create a Classroom Environment at Home

It helps if the family can create a classroom environment at home for the child to do his homework. This does not mean tearing down walls and recreating the classroom. Simple things such as a similar desk, or even setting up the materials the same way, will help to get the student started. Send home the students' pencil, scissors, and other materials needed to complete the homework. The environment may be different from the school's, but having consistent tools and other materials is helpful.

When children see that their sister or brother with autism also has homework, it helps them to see their siblings in a new light. This is a small but important step in their ongoing relationship.

Dog
6 year old

Chapter Nine

Activities

The Daily Grind

Structure the Day and Classroom Setting

Tightly structuring the day is important. People with autism do not always do well with unstructured time. Plan meaningful activities for every part of the day. The length of time for each activity will depend on the age and needs of the individual. Some students with autism have problems attending for even just a minute on a non-preferred activity, and yet they can spend hours on an activity that engages them.

Breaks are an important part of our lives, and teachers should teach break time strategies to students with autism. This will become a crucial part of their lives when they have to perform in the work place while on and off task.

You will find children with autism in many different classroom settings. Some students may be fully included within the general population with varying amounts of support. The support may be visual aids that they carry with them, like a schedule, or a calming device, like a stress ball. The support could also be a paraprofessional to assist the individual, a quiet place to go when needed, etc.

Some children with autism may spend part of the day in general education classes and part of the day in a special education class. Some students may spend the majority of their school day in a special education classroom.

The type of class the students with autism attend, the students' ages, and individual needs determine how many of the following activities fit into their day. Choose activities and design a day to fit the students' needs.

Individual activities are individual, and they vary from student to student. The teacher should develop activities for, and with, the individual. Therefore, the majority of the suggested activities in this section are group activities. These activities are important for several reasons:

- Group activities give students with autism much needed social skills practice. Many times these students want to interact with others but simply do not know how to do so in a socially acceptable manner. Other people often see their attempts at interaction as rude, mean, or simply bizarre.

- Group activities help desensitize children to contact with groups. Many people with autism experience tactile defensiveness and sensitivity to smells and/or sounds that make close contact a very uncomfortable experience. Many times you can handle these aversions in a systematic manner that reduces the anxiety. For example, if smell is a problem, you can control the type of soaps or perfumes people use. Sitting slightly away from the group and slowly moving in can help. Allowing children with autism to keep their space from the group while still participating is another acceptable way to be part of a group.

- Group activities provide strategies for dealing with unpredictable events that occur in everyday life. You can structure the activity within a group, but you can never control every little outcome. This leads to some interesting scenarios. You can help the person with autism deal with unpredictability with "on the job training."

- Group activities are bridges to the social world we live in, whether we experience autism or not.

Creating and Managing Activities

Never assume that students with autism cannot, or will not, do an activity, even if they have refused to do this particular activity every day. Observe children at play, and you will note that they do not automatically assume a person won't or can't do something. They plunge in with expectations of success. As Yoda said in *Star Wars*: "Do, or do not. There is no try." Children naturally emulate Yoda when it comes to play with their peers.

Allow an assistant to be in charge of structured activities whenever possible. You can take on assistant duties at these times. This is an excellent training experience for the teacher's assistant. It is also important for the students to be able to take instruction from more than one person.

When the teacher's assistant is comfortable in the teaching role, the teacher is free to visit students involved in inclusive classes or work one on one with a student. When the teacher is absent due to illness or other unexpected reasons, the assistant has had experience, and the class can continue with much needed consistency.

One activity will almost always lead to another one. Create your own activity sheets using the format in this book. When creating an activity sheet, make the instructions so clear that a stranger (such as a substitute teacher) can pick up the sheet and successfully conduct the activity.

Even though the goals listed on my activity sheets may appear obvious, it is easy to get wrapped up in the process of the activity and lose sight of the big picture. Have goals clearly thought out and written as a reminder of what the student is to accomplish. Busy work does not help individuals with autism any more than it does those without autism.

Have all props gathered and accessible before beginning the activity. A teacher may have a wonderful activity planned, but if she has to stop and leave the individual or group to gather materials, students can quickly lose interest due to lack of continuity. The students may find their own amusement in a flash, and it may not always be an acceptable one.

The Color of Autism: **John**

John had two favorite activities at school. One was flicking his fingers in front of his face and running from wall to wall. The other activity was following me around.

It was my first year of teaching children with autism. My fascination with autism was my strongest point. I did not have a clue as to how to teach these children.

I had to start somewhere with instruction, so I took a stab in the dark. I decided to teach John how to go to the door, turn the lights off, come back and sit down, and then, on cue, go back and turn on the lights.

After six weeks of daily "light off, light on" lessons, John did it! I was elated. I had him demonstrate his light skills to anyone who would watch. Then I turned the lesson over to a fellow teacher. John would not do it. He would only turn the lights off and on for me.

I tried the same lesson in a different classroom, and he would not, could not, do it. Only when I instructed him to go to the door and turn the lights off in the same classroom would he perform the feat.

When I thought of all the possible combinations of lights, people, and places for John to relearn the task, I was astounded. I had spent six weeks of John's life teaching him a pretty useless task.

Or had I? John had learned to listen and follow a command. We had learned to work together on a common goal. And, John was obviously proud of himself for accomplishing a task that I had made so important.

I was the one who learned the most from this lesson, however. I had spent the seven previous years teaching in an elementary school. Did I expect a second grader who was mastering second grade math to understand calculus? I had overlooked one of the most important tools a teacher has: building on what the child knows.

John did not know or care about the meaning of "lights" at this stage of his life. He did not care if they were on or if they were off. I was trying to teach him to do this task when he heard a command in a language that he was obviously struggling to understand. John had acted out the command but could not transfer the skill to another setting.

For John, this was an isolated event. As I grasped the complexities of John and his autism, I had to admire his ability to learn a task that must have been insurmountable and meaningless to him. John and I had developed a close student/ teacher bond, and I am sure that like many other elementary students, he really wanted to please his teacher.

Unfortunately, John's teacher had not been wise enough to select a lesson that was relevant for him and one that he could build on to learn other skills. John could not express his basic wants and needs. He could not dress or undress himself or take care of his personal hygiene.

I spent days beating myself up over my obvious ignorance, but then I realized that I was on the right path. I had just taken a detour. It had been an enlightening detour, however.

I observed John for several days, making notes of what appeared to be relevant for him. Once we began working on basic skills at John's level, we saw progress. John had a precarious grasp on controlling his environment.

I learned a great deal from my work with John. He taught me that the student has to lead the way. I learned to sit back, observe, and note how each student responds to the environment. How do the students respond to pleasure, pain, and frustration? Is the child curious? What repetitious behaviors does the child display? How can you take those behaviors and turn them into teaching tools?

If the person is fascinated with lights, find toys and teaching tools that use lights to teach and then gradually move away from the lights. If the child is fascinated with wheels, use wheels to teach basic shapes.

John also taught me that repetition is an important way that individuals with autism can master a skill. Once the skill is apparently mastered, however, one cannot assume that the person will retain the skill without ongoing reinforcement and practice. Have you learned a foreign language and then not used it for several years? You probably need a refresher course.

John taught me to vary the location to make sure the person with autism can learn to transfer the skill from one place to another. He taught me to beware of cues. A person with autism can appear to have learned a skill when, in reality, he has learned to respond to a cue and cannot perform the task without the cue.

I learned that all people with autism are not alike. John had his own personality, likes and dislikes, and learning style. John was not autism; he was a young man with autism.

John was a great teacher, and I was a willing student. Thanks, John!

Develop a Classroom Schedule

The following is a sample weekly schedule for the classroom. Display your schedule in the classroom. Duplicate it, cut it into daily strips, put it in book form, and send a copy home with each student. The schedule will give the parent information that they can use to communicate with their child about the school day. The schedule should not replace a daily communication log between parent and teacher; it is a supplement. You can customize the weekly schedule and duration of activities to fit the age, individual learning styles, ability levels, etc.

The Week at a Glance
Sample Schedule

MONDAY	TUESDAY	WEDNESDAY	THURSDAY	FRIDAY
Book bag, coat, etc.a.m.	Book bag, coat, etc.a.m.	Book bag, coat, etc.a.m.	Book bag, coat, etc.a.m.	Book bag, coat, etc.a.m.
Aerobics	Aerobics	Aerobics	Aerobics	Aerobics
Circle I – Greetings	Circle I – Greetings	Circle I – Greetings	Circle I – Greetings	Circle I – Greetings
Calendar	Gym with Mr. Leap	Calendar	Calendar	Gym with Mr. Leap
Music with Mrs. Harp	Music with Mrs. Harp	Reading I, II, or III	Arts & Crafts	Reading I, II, or III
Make a Book	Reading I, II, or III	Make a Book	Library with Mrs. Book	Make a Book
LUNCH	LUNCH	LUNCH	LUNCH	LUNCH
Break or recess	Break or recess	Break or recess	Break or recess	Break or recess
Circle II – cassette CD	Academics	Academics	Academics	Academics
Academics	Library with Mrs. Book	Computer Lab	Computer Lab	Computer Lab
Reading I, II, or III	Calendar	Group speech	Reading I, II, or III	Reading I, II, or III
Snack/Clean up	Snack/Clean up	Snack/Clean up	Snack/Clean up	Snack/Clean up
Arts & Crafts	Arts & Crafts	Arts & Crafts	Arts & Crafts	Arts & Crafts
Choices	Circle II – cassette CD	Tea Time with the King & Queen	Choices	Circle II – cassette CD
Book bag p.m. Dismissal	Book bag p.m. Dismissal	Book bag p.m. Dismissal	Book bag p.m. Dismissal	Book bag p.m. Dismissal

Each activity from this schedule is outlined in detail in the following pages.

Activities List

1. Book bag, coat, etc. a.m.
2. Aerobics
3. Circle I – Greetings
4. Circle II – Cassette/CD
5. Calendar
6. Academics
7. Music with Mrs. Harp
8. Library with Mrs. Book
9. Gym with Mr. Leap
10. Computer Lab
11. Reading I – Big Book & Tape
12. Reading II – Reading With a Friend
13. Reading III – Read-In
14. LUNCH
15. Break or Recess
16. Arts & Crafts
17. Choices
18. Snack
19. Clean up
20. Tea Time with the King and Queen
21. Make a Book
22. Book bag, coat, etc., p.m.

When structuring the activities, use everything you know about the person with autism—learning style, sensory issues, etc., and individualize as much as possible.

Remember these are only suggestions. Use what works with your students and within your environment. Adapt activities to age-appropriate levels.

Activities from Sample Daily Schedule

Activity   Estimated Time Required

Book bag, coat, etc.   5 minutes
Putting away in a.m.

Goal(s)

♦ Caring for personal property
♦ Following verbal instruction/auditory processing
♦ Following written/picture instruction
♦ Independence

Props

Book bag
Hook
Area labeled with student's name

Cues – See *The Fine Art of Cueing*

Directions

Students enter the room and check their schedule to determine that it is time to put things away and get ready for the day. Post the students' names by their personal space for coats and backpacks. When labeling the environment, use consistent print.

Some students have notebooks, homework, or other materials that they need to turn in before starting class. Have a labeled basket or tray in a designated spot for notebooks and another one for homework.

Once the students have put their belongings in the appropriate place, they should check their individual schedules and start their day.

Spin Offs

The students should be responsible for picking up toys, putting materials away, etc. Individuals with autism often will drop items when they move to a new activity. (Reminds you of teenagers, doesn't it?) Always have the student pick up dropped items and put them in their proper place. Provide visual cues when possible. Do not shrug your shoulders, sigh, and put the materials away for the student.

Activity	Estimated Time Required
Aerobics	20–30 minutes

Goal(s)

Awareness of Body in Space

♦ Following verbal instruction/auditory processing
♦ Following visual cues/modeling movements of others
♦ Physical conditioning
♦ Increased stamina
♦ Working as a member of a group

Props

Aerobic routine – CD or tape
Area rug/tape to provide a boundary. Students stay within boundaries during aerobics.

Cues – See *The Fine Art of Cueing*

Directions

Students check their schedules and determine it is time for aerobics. Everyone assembles in the designated area. The designated area could be an area rug (round rugs work well), tape on the floor, a small room, etc. (It may take many reminders for the children to stay on the rug, inside the tape, etc., but you are reinforcing basic directional concepts.) Start the CD or tape.

Important: Do not talk during the routine. Do not give verbal cues. Let the students follow the verbal cues from the recording and the visual cues from the others doing the routine. Try to keep everyone facing forward in a circle so that they can see each other.

Talking and directing may confuse students who have problems with over stimulation and/or auditory processing. If a student requires hand-over-hand cueing, stand behind the student to assist. This allows the student the opportunity to visually attend to others doing the aerobics routine.

Spin Offs

- You can also use some of the numerous videotapes; however, I prefer the audio routines in order to increase auditory processing and imitation of visual cues.

- There are seated aerobic routines created for people who are wheelchair-bound. I have found these beneficial for students who are having a bad day, or just for a change of pace.

- Several different routines add variety; however, use the same routine often enough for everyone to learn. Predictability is important to individuals with autism. The more you expose the students to a routine, the better they will learn to follow it.

- Send a copy of the routine home for the student to do with friends and family.

The Color of Autism: **Timmy**

Timmy would not stay on the carpet that we used as a boundary for aerobics. Someone always had to bring Timmy back to the carpet.

After three weeks of daily aerobics, in which Timmy did not participate and continually left the area, we noticed that he was doing different parts of the aerobics routine at other times. Timmy's mother reported that he was doing aerobics in the evening.

We continued to include Timmy in aerobics and bring him back to the group when he escaped. A month passed before Timmy started doing aerobics with the group. At first he only did an isolated movement here and there, but eventually he did entire segments.

By the end of the first semester, Timmy was doing the entire set with the group. He became the role model for our peer tutors. He also continued to do aerobics throughout the day, without instruction or music. We made him a copy of the routine to take home, and the whole family joined Timmy for an evening aerobics session.

Activity	**Estimated Time Required**
Circle I	30 minutes

Goal(s)

◆ Socialization
◆ Appropriate greetings
◆ Appropriate reciprocation of greetings
◆ Following visual cues/modeling movements of others
◆ Following verbal instruction/auditory processing
◆ Working as a member of a group
◆ Turn taking

Props

Typical peers are beneficial. I used a ratio of one student without autism for every student with autism. Provide name cards.

Cues – See *The Fine Art of Cueing*

Directions

Students check their schedules and determine that it is time for Circle. They sit in a semi-circle or circle. This allows everyone to be visible.

One student begins. He stands, shakes everyone's hand, and says, "Hello" or "Good Morning" with the person's name. Students with autism are given ample time to respond.

The greeter can use a name card with students without speech. The student can point to the greeter's name. If the student uses a communication device, use it for this activity. Everyone takes a turn with as much support as needed.

Spin Offs

- Students can sing their greeting and their response.

- Have a "Be Creative with Your Greeting" day.

- Use no spoken language. Have everyone communicate in an alternate manner.

- Give extra information or request extra information. Example: "Hi, I am a _____(boy or girl). Are you a boy or girl?" "Hello, I am wearing a blue dress. What color is your _____ (shirt, pants, dress, etc.)?"

Activity	**Estimated Time Required**
Circle II - Cassette/CD	30 minutes

Goal(s)

♦ Following verbal instruction/auditory processing
♦ Working as a member of a group
♦ Following visual cues/modeling movements of others

Props

Audio cassettes or CDs
One cassette or CD for each routine
Suggestions: Finger plays, number songs, alphabet songs, weather songs, phonics

Cues – See *The Fine Art of Cueing*

Directions

Students check their schedules and determine that it is time for Circle II. Use a different routine for each day of the week.

Taped, instead of teacher-directed, routines benefit students with autism because of their consistency. Do not to talk while the audio cassette/CD is playing. Individuals with autism may have difficulty attending to more than one stimulus at a time.

Spin Offs

- Use interactive videos, such as sing-alongs.

- Preview many different recordings. Libraries are excellent resources. Record a series of the students' favorite selections by theme.

- In addition to becoming part of the students' day, these routines are lifesavers for emergency situations when you need a structured block of time in a jiffy.

Activities from Daily Schedule

Activity	Estimated Time Required
Calendar	5 minutes per student

Goal(s)

♦ Reading
♦ Sequencing
♦ Counting
♦ Order of days of week
♦ Order of months of year
♦ Name recognition
♦ Turn taking

Props

Large calendar
Number squares to fit squares on calendar
Days of week to fit calendar
Months of year to fit on top of calendar

Cues – See *The Fine Art of Cueing*

Directions

Students check their schedules and determine that it is time for Calendar. One student affixes the number for the current day and then counts to that day from number one. Use hand over hand if necessary. The student recites days of the week and points his finger to the correct day. "Today is _____. Yesterday was _____. Tomorrow will be _____.

You can list the months down the side of the calendar. The student recites months while touching each month. When the student comes to the current month, it should be missing from the side and affixed to the top of the calendar. The student points to the current month. Non-verbal students can point or use a communication device.

Each student takes a turn at counting and reciting days of the week and months. Groups of two or three are manageable. While a small group is doing Calendar, the rest of the class can be doing a cassette/CD activity with a teacher's assistant.

Spin Offs

- Add bits of information such as; "I am a _____ (boy or girl). My address is _____. My phone number is _____. It is _____ (spring, summer, winter, fall)."

Activity	Estimated Time Required
Academics	Individual

Tips on Structuring Academics

Use visual cues whenever possible. Provide a visual beginning and ending to each assignment.

Some students need tubs/baskets to hold their work. Each tub should hold only one assignment. Have one tub/basket for the assignment and another for the finished work. Place the beginning work tub/baskets on the students' right and the finished work tub/basket on the students' left.

• Other students can use folders to hold assignments.

> Mark the left side of the folder with the words "Begin" or "Start." This side of the folder will hold the assignment. Mark the right side of the folder "Completed" or "Finished." The student places the completed assignment in the right side.

• Have all materials needed to complete each assignment close at hand.

> Students who use the tub/basket method can have all the materials needed for the assignment right in the tub/basket.

• Give only enough work to complete in a designated amount of time.

> Many individuals with autism need to finish an assignment before moving on to the next task. If they finish before the allotted time, they can always choose a free-time activity.

- Each student should have a designated place to work, such as a desk or table.

- Some individuals need a calm, quiet area to work. You can create study areas with bookcases, dividers, or study carrels.

- Many young students with autism do not want to hold things like a pencil, crayon, marker, or scissors.

  If the use of these implements is a daily part of the students' schedules, they will soon become accustomed to the implements and make progress. Do not wait until they are "ready" because they may never be ready without intervention.

- Include a few favorite, mastered tasks when introducing a new task.

- See *The Fine Art of Cueing*

Activities from Daily Schedule

Activity	Estimated Time Required
Music with Mrs. Harp Adapt time to individual needs	Block of time scheduled by school

Goal(s)

♦ When students with autism go to a music class with typical peers, classroom and music teachers should write the goals the student is to accomplish in that class. For some students, the goals may be the same as any other student. However, other students may have a goal for sitting for a certain amount of time. Another student may have the goal of tolerating the closeness of other students. Of course, the goals should be student-specific.

Props

The student with autism may or may not require special equipment in music class. One student may need earplugs when the students play the instruments, another student may need a comfortable chair, and still another student may need to carry a certain item to make him feel secure when away from homeroom.

Cues – See *The Fine Art of Cueing*

Directions

Students check their schedules and determine that it is time for Music. Start with the expectation for the class as a whole and adapt for the individual with autism. Remember: do not fix what is not broken.

Spin Offs

- Incorporate music into the classroom. The bottle band is a favorite music activity. Fill empty, plastic bottles with various materials like feathers, rocks, sand, dirt, marbles, sparkles, water, ribbon, mud, or a combination of materials. Glue the lids on, and you have marvelous rattles that make different sounds.

- Shake the bottles slowly. Shake the bottles fast. Shake the bottles to a count. Shake them high. Shake them low. Have one student shake his bottle over his head, behind his back, etc., and let the other students copy the movements.

Activities from Daily Schedule

Activity   Estimated Time Required

Library with Mrs. Book   20–30 minutes

Goal(s)

- ♦ Utilizing books for leisure time
- ♦ Utilizing books for information
- ♦ Making choices
- ♦ Following rules

Props

Perhaps give students tickets to represent the number of books they may check out.

Cues – See *The Fine Art of Cueing*

Directions

Students check their schedules and determine that it is time for Library. Students follow the library rules that the school has set. Make adaptations for individuals as needed.

Spin Offs

- Have a library in the classroom to teach students the appropriate way to handle books.

- Books on tape are another way for students to enjoy books.

- A trip to the local library is a worthwhile adventure. It can help students transfer skills to a community setting.

Activities from Daily Schedule

Activity	Estimated Time Required
Gym with Mr. Leaf	Block of time scheduled by school

Goal(s)

♦ When individuals with autism go to a gym class, share the students goals with the gym teacher and the peers who will be working with them. Many students with autism will have the same goals as everyone else in the class; however, some students may need accommodations such as length of time for activities or specific sensory needs.

Props

The individual with autism may or may not require special equipment in a gym class. Some props that may be beneficial are a favorite ball when playing ball games or a special place to be while in the gym.

Cues – See *The Fine Art of Cueing*

Directions

Students check their schedules and determine that it is time for gym. Break down the directions for the gym activities into smaller segments. Use picture or word sequence cards if necessary.

Practice the gym activities at other times during the day. You can give students individual visual-cue cards for various activities. For example, when running laps, the students could receive three tickets each, and every time they make a lap, they would drop one ticket in a basket. When the tickets are gone, the students are finished.

Individuals with autism may enjoy the repetition of organized sports. Do not leave them out if they are able to do only a part of the game. Allow them to do whatever part is comfortable for them, and build skills needed for the total game over a period of time.

Spin Offs

- Send a description of the activities home for homework.

- Use parts of activities at recess. For example, if the activity is kickball, work on just kicking the ball.

- Videotape the activity for the student to watch at home or school.

Activities from Daily Schedule

Activity	Estimated Time Required
Computer Lab	Varies

The following is one application of computers for a student with autism.

The Color of Autism: **Jill**

Jill had struggled with augmentative communication the entire school year. She had speech but did not initiate or go beyond two-word responses. She had attempted to use picture wallets, communication boards, a typewriter, and several speaking devices. Jill's family wanted her to be able to tell about her school day, and none of the methods we had tried were successful in achieving this particular goal.

Jill's computer skills were growing. She was doing schoolwork on the computer and was beginning to use it to express herself as well.

We decided to utilize her computer skills to help her share her day at school with her family. The last assignment on her schedule was: **Computer. Dear Mom and Dad**.

At first we gave her a format to follow. The following is a sample of what would be on the computer screen when Jill sat down. She was to fill in the blanks.

Date: _____

Dear Mom and Dad,

Today I went to _____ **class and** _____

class.

For lunch, I had _____**and**

_____**and**_____ **. I**

drank _____**.**

I played with _____ **during recess.**

Love,

At first, Jill just filled in the blanks when cued to do so. Eventually, we removed the sentences. Jill continued to follow the same format, even when the sentences and blanks were no longer there.

Jill began adding new information. One day a bee stung her on the playground. She typed "Bee bit." Another time she went to a dance recital with her class, and she added, "pretty dance." This new line of communication pleased Jill's parents. They especially liked that Jill gave the information and not a third party. Jill's note provided a new line of communication with her parents. The communication continued to grow as the school year went on.

Activity	Estimated Time Required
Reading I	15–30 minutes
Story Strip & Tape	

Goal(s)

♦ Reading for pleasure
♦ Reading for information
♦ Reading with another person
♦ Reading independently
♦ Following verbal instruction/auditory processing
♦ Sharing

Props

BIG Story book (can be found at libraries)
Corresponding audio cassette or CD

Cues – See *The Fine Art of Cueing*

Directions

Students check their schedule and determine that it is time for reading. This can be an independent or group activity. The students listen to the story on tape and follow along in the book.

Spin Offs

• Our BIG books had familiar children's stories. The students became so familiar with the stories that we acted out plays about the stories.

• The students became very attached to the books and loved to look at them while lying on the floor. Turning pages was a problem for some children, so we created the strip method. Here is what we did:

> We wrote stories about the students. We used bits and pieces that they told us during Circle Time and

embellished this information into a simple story. We printed the story on a long strip of paper and then laminated the paper. We recorded the story on audio cassette. Students selected these stories during Reading I or free time. The favorite method for listening was to unroll the story on the floor and sometimes follow along or even roll on the story itself.

The Color of Autism: **Kevin**

When it was time for Reading I – BIG Book, Kevin would squeeze his body between the teacher and the book and get his face very close to the type. He followed intently with the audiotape. None of the other students could see around Kevin's head. If we moved Kevin back, he would cry.

One day, a minor crisis occurred and I had to leave the group quickly. When I returned, Kevin was in the teacher's chair, holding the BIG book for the other students. He was turning the pages at the appropriate time and giving cues to pay attention by calling the children's names.

<u>Activity</u>	<u>Estimated Time Required</u>
Reading II	15–30 minutes
Reading with a Friend	

<u>Goal(s)</u>

♦ Reading for pleasure
♦ Reading for information
♦ Reading with another person
♦ Following verbal instruction/auditory processing
♦ Taking turns
♦ Choosing a partner
♦ Sharing

<u>Props</u>

Book appropriate for age level and interest
Peer without autism
Quiet area

<u>Cues – See *The Fine Art of Cueing*</u>

<u>Directions</u>

Students check their schedules and determine that it is time for Reading II. Begin in the circle area with the students sitting. Have students select a partner. Alternate the selection between student without autism and the student with autism.

Students select their books from the room library, school library, home library, etc. Students select their own spot in the room or hall, wherever they feel comfortable reading. Some students like to sit or lie on the floor, others do not. Make room for individual styles and sensory preferences. Some individuals with autism may not want to look at the book while the other person is reading. Or, they may want to touch the book while the other person is reading.

The person with autism may or may not be able to read. They may be able to read a few words, or they may have the entire book memorized. They may want to touch the words, but not read them.

Encourage the students to finish the entire book if possible, or at least finish a chapter.

Spin Offs

- Send a book home for homework. Suggest that the student read with a sibling or parent.

- The reader can tape the book for the other person to listen to later.

- Reading partners can take turns with words, sentences, paragraphs, or pages.

Activity   Estimated Time Required

Reading III   10–15 minutes
Read-In

Goal(s)

♦ Reading for pleasure
♦ Reading for information
♦ Reading independently
♦ Developing attention span
♦ Developing an inclusive activity

Props

Favorite books
More books than students
Books at appropriate age level
Books at appropriate level of interest
Timer

Cues – See *The Fine Art of Cueing*

Directions

Students check their schedules and determine that it is time for Reading III. Create a quiet classroom environment.

Everyone chooses a book. Set a timer for a predetermined amount of time. Start with short periods of time and increase gradually with each reading session.

The individual with autism may want to spend time with a book that many of us would not consider reading. For example, he or she may sniff or touch the pages. Credit is given for any type of communing with his or her book.

Spin Offs

- Many schools have "read-ins" where the entire school spends a certain amount of time with books.

- Encourage parents to have read-ins with the entire family.

- The student with autism may want to select a magazine, phone book, newspaper, comic book, etc. instead of a traditional book.

Activity   Estimated Time Required

Lunch   Block of time scheduled by school
           Adapt time to individual needs

Goal(s)

♦ Independence
♦ Etiquette
♦ Fine motor skills
♦ Waiting when finished
♦ Cleaning up

Props

A lunch ticket with the student's name
A wallet or purse
Choice cards

Cues – See *The Fine Art of Cueing*

Directions

Students check their schedules and see that it is time for lunch. The lunch tickets may be a part of the schedule. When the students check their schedules, they take off the lunch ticket and carry it to the lunchroom. At my last school, the children needed to tell the lunch cashier their name as they went through the line. The tickets worked well for students who did not have language or needed more processing time in order to give their names. The students with adequate language did not want to be left out and demanded tickets, so all the students had a ticket.

In some elementary schools, and most secondary schools, students have a choice at lunchtime. Have students make selections from the cafeteria menu before going to the lunchroom. The selections can be put on cards and handed to the appropriate person.

Spin Offs

I do not encourage secluding individuals with autism from their peers. However, some students may not be able to handle the busy confusion of a lunchroom. They should be allowed to experience the lunchroom by perhaps waiting outside while another person gets the lunch for them. Then they can take their lunch to a quieter place. They could work up to going into the lunchroom, retrieving their own lunch, and bringing it back to a quiet area. A peer could eat lunch with the student with autism in the quiet area. Then another peer can go, and then another, until several children are in the quiet area.

A child with autism may go to the cafeteria when it is quiet and have a snack. Do not allow the child to stay in the quiet area. Gradually desensitize him or her to the busy lunchroom until he or she can comfortably join the peers there. Skills learned at lunchtime can be carried over to home and community.

Activities from Daily Schedule

Activity   ## Estimated Time Required

Break/recess   20 minutes

Goal(s)

♦ Appropriate use of free time
♦ Use of vending machines
♦ Use of restrooms
♦ Returning from break in a timely fashion
♦ Appropriate interaction with others
♦ Identifying break area
♦ Telling time
♦ Reading environmental cues
♦ Making appropriate choices

Props

Break area
Coins for vending machine
Materials for use during break (games, toys, books, etc.)
Clock or watch

Cues – See *The Fine Art of Cueing*

Directions

Students check their schedules and determine that it is time for a break or recess. Provide materials for scheduled breaks, such as toys, books, games, etc. Students need to have a way to ask for a break during other activities. This could be by simply asking or using a communication device. The individual needs to know how long the break should be. Provide a way to determine that the break is over: a timer, watch alarm, clock, etc.

When young children with autism are at recess, have a peer without autism to help them negotiate all of the ins and outs of recess. Usually group games are involved, as well as lining up on cue and returning to the school.

Spin Offs

- For students with autism who do not easily join other children at play, we developed *Shadow Play*. The peers without autism followed the child and imitated his or her play.

- Friends made during breaks and recess may become friends outside of school.

- Break skills may be transferable to the work environment.

Activities from Daily Schedule

Activity   Estimated Time Required

Arts & Crafts   Depends on project
May require more than one session

Goal(s)

♦ Developing a hobby
♦ Cause and effect
♦ Working as a member of a group
♦ Following verbal instructions/auditory processing
♦ Fine motor skills

Props

Depends on project

Cues – See *The Fine Art of Cueing*

Directions

Students check their schedule and determine that it is time for arts and crafts.

Spin Offs

For suggestions see:
Reaching the Child with Autism through Art, Toni Flowers, 1992, Published by Future Horizons, Inc., 721 W. Abram Street, Arlington, Texas 76013,
Phone: 800-489-0727.

Activity   Estimated Time Required

Choices   30 minutes

Goal(s)

- ◆ Making choices
- ◆ Working as a member of a group
- ◆ Following through with a choice
- ◆ Increasing time on task
- ◆ Cause and effect

Props

Choice board – with removable pictures of the various choices available

Choice cards - can be photographs, line drawings, or word cards to reflect choices

Choice station (stations set up with various choices that are reflected in the choice board)
Timer

Cues – See *The Fine Art of Cueing*

Directions

Students check their schedules and determine that it is time for Choices. Place the choice board in front of the group. The board should have the various choices on cards attached by Velcro®, paper clips, etc. The students should be able to easily remove the cards.

When it is the students' turn, they go to the choice board and select an activity. There should be a designated spot at the choice station for the students to place their cards.

Once the students have made their choices and are at the choice station, set the timer for a certain period of time, depending on the students' attention spans. A good rule of thumb is to set the timer to accommodate the student with the shortest attention span.

The students stay on task until the timer goes off. They can go back to the choice board and select another choice card, and the process begins again.

Spin Offs – Suggestions for Choice Stations

- Dress up – have a trunk full of fun clothes and shoes

- Water or sand table

- Bubbles

- Blocks

- Table games that require two or more

- Remote control items

- Handheld video games

Activity	**Estimated Time Required**
Tea Time with the King & Queen	20–30 minutes

Goal(s)

◆ Social interaction
◆ Imaginative play
◆ Etiquette
◆ Working as a member of a group
◆ Sharing
◆ Taking turns

Props

Two crowns. One for the King and one for the Queen

Tea cups, saucers, tea, teapot

Small plates

Napkins

Place mats

Platter

Small cookies or crackers

Basket

Name cards

Cues – See *The Fine Art of Cueing*

Directions

Students check their schedules and determine that it is time for tea. Participants' name cards are in the "royal basket." Someone draws cards to determine who is to be the King and who is to be the Queen. The teacher, assistant, or former King and Queen present the new members of the royalty with crowns.

The King and Queen sit at the head of the table. They each select an attendant. The attendants stand behind the royal couple.

Make the herbal tea beforehand so that it can cool. The Queen directs her attendant to give each humble participant a place mat, teacup, saucer, napkin, and small plate.

The teacher, assistant, or student has already prepared a platter of cookies and crackers. The Queen directs her attendant to give her the platter. She offers each person a designated amount of cookies. "Take one cookie, please," or "Take two crackers, please." The King and his attendant remind students of their manners. Students have to address the King and Queen with, "Yes, your Highness," "No, your Highness," or "Thank you, your Highness." As the students leave the table, they curtsey or bow to the King and Queen.

Spin Offs

- Have teatime with favorite storybook characters, television personalities, characters from movies, etc., instead of with the King and Queen.

- Students may make "fancy" place mats in arts and crafts, using doilies, sparkles, etc. Laminate place mats for longer use.

Activity	Estimated Time Required
Snack	30 minutes

Goal(s)

♦ Etiquette
♦ Fine motor (pouring, stirring, use of utensils)
♦ Communication
♦ Taking turns
♦ Sharing
♦ Working as a member of a group

Props

Dishes (color cue each person's cup and plate. One person can have red, another one blue, etc.)

Snack items

Choice cards – cards with pictures or picture with identifying word of snack items

Pitcher

Drink

Cues – See *The Fine Art of Cueing*

Directions

Students check their schedules and see that it is time for a snack. After students are seated, give them a card identifying what utensils they will need for the day's snack. If only a cup is needed, give them a cup card. If the cup and plate are needed, give the students the cup card and the plate card.

The students take their cards to a designated area for dishes (a bookcase works nicely) and find their name cards. Their personal dishes should be in the spot with their name card. If the student only needs the cup, he or she exchanges the cup card for his or her cup and returns to the table.

When all of the students have the appropriate dishes, the teacher introduces the snacks by showing the choice cards. There might be a choice of two or more snacks, or just one.

Students need to communicate their desire for a snack. They may point to the choice card, use an augmentative device, use sign language, use language, etc. No one should receive a snack, however, without attempting to communicate that they want a snack.

All the students pour their own drinks. If spills occur, the student cleans up the spill with whatever assistance is needed.

Spin Offs

- Students who respond to verbal commands do not need to use the cards; however, many children who do not need the cards will ask for them.

- Have a picnic using the same methods.

- Assign a student to be the teacher for a day.

Activity	**Estimated Time Required**
Clean up (from snack)	Depends on number of students

Goal(s)

♦ Independence
♦ Following a sequence (use visual sequence strips if necessary)
♦ Cause and effect

Props

Dishes

Sink, dish soap, cloth or sponge

Drainer, dish towel

Cues – See *The Fine Art of Cueing*

Directions

Students check their schedules and see that it is time to clean up. Have sequence strips ready. A sequence strip is a pictorial "how-to" using pictures. The pictures are arranged in left-to-right or top-to-bottom order. Arrange them in the sequence of the activity. The pictures may be very involved or very simple, depending on the level of need. For washing dishes, the strip might have picture cards showing:

1. Filling sink with water
2. Adding dish soap
3. Putting dishes in water
4. Washing dishes
5. Putting dishes in rack
6. Drying dishes
7. Putting dishes away

Spin Offs

- If available, use the dishwasher.

- Older students may have a job washing dishes in the school cafeteria.

- Send homework assignment to do dishes. Send the sequence strip, if necessary.

The Color of Autism: **Jeannie**

Jeannie's mother wanted her to help rake leaves. Jeannie would take the rake from her mother, take one swipe at the leaves, drop the rake, and begin twiddling a leaf. No matter what incentive her mother offered, Jeannie would not go beyond the initial swipe.

Jeannie's mother asked me for advice. We decided to try visual cues for Jeannie. The sequence strips were becoming successful at school, but sometimes Jeannie needed visual cues within an activity.

We created a sequence chart of raking leaves. We used a hula-hoop to accentuate a pile of leaves. We asked Jeannie to put all the leaves that were inside the hoop into a bag. This worked, but Jeannie was still not raking the leaves.

Next, we used a garden hose to create an even bigger circle. Using the sequence strip, Jeannie was to rake the leaves that were inside the hose into a pile and then bag the leaves. After much demonstration and rehearsal, Jeannie would rake the leaves that were inside the hose circle, but bagging was another story. She would look at the sequence strip, pick up one handful of leaves, and be done with it.

We then gave Jeannie two cards; each card had a picture of a full leaf bag. She was to fill a bag for each card. This did the trick. When we wanted her to fill more than two bags, we gave her the required amount of cards. She would not fill one bag more or less than her cards. For some reason, she would not go over five, but she was raking and filling bags with the help of her visual aids. Jeannie's mother applied this system to other household chores with varying success.

Activity   Estimated Time Required

Make a Book   30 minutes per session
Example: Number Book

Goal(s)

♦ Work as a member of a group
♦ Fine motor skills
♦ Sequencing pages
♦ Making choices
♦ Following verbal directions/auditory processing

Props

Per book:

10 pieces of 8" x 11" construction paper with outline of gumball machine reproduced on each page

2 pieces of colored construction paper for cover

Round stickers, assorted colors for gumballs

Stapler

Marker

Paper clips (one for each student)

Cues – See *The Fine Art of Cueing*

Directions

Students check their schedule and determine that it is time for Make a Book.

Session I: Talk about making a book. Show several books from the library. Explain that this will be a number book. Read a number book to the students. There will be one sticker (gumball) on the first page, two on the second page, etc. The students can take the completed book home to share with family.

Session II: Students count 10 pieces of white construction paper (with help, if needed). The students secure the construction paper with a paper clip (good fine motor skill). They choose colors of construction paper for the front and back of the book. Students remove paper clips and staple front and back cover to the 10 pieces of paper. They number pages at the bottom of the white construction paper, 1 to 10. Make tracing pattern or use hand-over-hand assistance as needed. Students put names on the front of the book. If needed, use same assistance as in numbering.

Session III: One student gives gumball books to appropriate students by reading the name on the front of the books. Students open to page one and put one sticker inside the gumball machine. They count the gumball, while pointing to it, to staff or peer helper.

Students continue to place appropriate number of gumballs inside the gumball machine until all ten pages are complete. They continue to count while pointing to each page.

Spin Offs

* Seasonal books

* Holidays

* ME books about family, pets, friends, etc. A ME book can be sent home empty for the student to complete with the family and brought back to school to share.

* Books of special interest

* Books dictated to teacher by student, then illustrated by student

* Make a Book can become homework, to be read to the family, or family to read to child

Activity	Estimated Time Required
Book bag/coat p.m.	5 minutes

Goal(s)

♦ Caring for personal property
♦ Following verbal instruction/auditory processing
♦ Following written/picture instruction
♦ Independence

Props

Book bag

Hook

Area labeled with student's name

Cues – See *The Fine Art of Cueing*

Directions

Students check their schedule and decide that it is time to get their book bags, coats, etc. and get ready to go home.

The student's name should be by his or her personal space for coats and backpacks. When labeling the environment, use consistent print throughout.

Some students have notebooks, homework, or other materials that they need to gather and put in their book bag before leaving school. Have a labeled basket or tray in a designated spot for notebooks and another one for homework.

Once the students have gathered their belongings and are ready to go home, they should go to the transition place and prepare to leave.

Spin Offs

- Make the students responsible for picking up toys, putting materials away, etc. Individuals with autism will drop items when they move on to a new activity. Again, always have the student pick up dropped items and put them in their proper place. Provide visual cues when possible. Do not shrug your shoulders, sigh, and put the materials away for the student. Provide needed support, and be prepared to back off and let the student do for himself.

Activities from Daily Schedule

- Make an ongoing video of the students. Show it weekly.

- Use large appliance boxes to create trains, space ships, houses, etc.

- Use large appliance boxes to create environments, such as a color environment. Cut windows in the box and cover with colored see-through film. Use a different color for each window.

- Make "feely" boxes with different textured items inside. Make the hole big enough to stick your hand into the box.

- Create plays using current reading material. Yes, it can be done. Requires lots and lots of repetition, but the end result is a hoot.

- Cook often.

- Sit back to back with a partner. Link arms and try to stand up.

- Play shopping with in-room grocery store items. Uses number and reading skills. Also uses imagination.

- Use commercial game boards and adapt to the individual.

- Adapt Bingo to numerous topics, such as

    Names of students
    Photographs of students
    Pictures of families
    Pictures of school staff
    Pictures of students' pets
    Favorite foods
    Favorite songs

- Make music daily — or at least make organized noise.

- Tape familiar sounds and play *What's That Sound* game.

- Stage parties with student participation in all aspects of planning.

- Experience nature. Hike, swim, camp, dance under the stars. Do flower arranging. Make things from found items such as, sticks, rocks, dirt, etc.

- Incorporate sensory activities whenever possible. Experience sand, rice, beans, shaving cream, and pudding in a way different from that intended on label.

- Play in the rain.

- Build a snowman. Paint your snowman with water colors.

- Play classical music.

- Mix up everyone's shoes and find your own.

- Play hot potato with different items such as balls, shoes, hats, etc.

- Play with a parachute.

- Shred a big pile of newspaper and take turns covering each other up. Let it rain newspaper. Turn the shreds into art projects. Make the clean-up a part of the activity.

- Play with flashlights in a darkened room.

- Play in dry leaves.

- Adapt familiar games such as *Musical Name Chairs*. In this game, the chairs are labeled with the individuals' names. When the music stops, the child sits in his own chair. No chairs are removed. Everyone is a winner.

• Laugh often.

The Color of Autism: **Travis**

My mother always welcomed my students into her home. I began taking my students to her house for Sunday dinners when I was teaching "normal" students in elementary school. The tradition continued when I began teaching children with autism. To my mother, kids were kids.

One day, my mother and I took my son Josh, who was 1-year-old, and one of my students with autism, Travis, to the Children's Museum. I pushed Joshua in his stroller, with my mother and Travis close behind. My mother and Travis were old buddies. She had kept him for a weekend when his parents had gone out of town.

I was surprised, but not concerned, when I turned around and Mom and Travis were nowhere to be seen. I called for them, but got no response. I retraced our steps to the car, thinking my mother or Travis had forgotten something. There was no sign of them anywhere. I began calling for her louder and louder, my voice rising with concern.

I heard a small voice coming from the hedges that surrounded the museum. In a soft voice Mom called out, "Toni." "Mom," I called, as I searched the hedges, pulling the stroller with Josh close behind. I saw a hand go up. "Over here," she said. I rolled Josh to the up-stretched arm, and when I parted the hedges, there were Mom and Travis.

Travis was sitting on the ground as close to the building as he could get. He had a firm hold on my mother's pants. "Help," my mother said in a whisper. She had seen the small group gathering to watch this unusual event. "I don't want these people to think I'm hurting him."

I held on to the stroller with one hand and removed Travis's hand from her pants with the other. "I'll trade you," I said. My mother said she didn't want to face the crowd, but she took the stroller, and I entered the hedge.

Travis looked terrified. I talked to him. He refused to leave. I offered him his favorite treat from the snack bar, but he still refused to leave. I took a deep breath and took both of his hands in mine and pulled him to his feet. Then I quickly pulled him out of the hedges, put my arm around him, and without stopping, I told my mother to follow. We walked quickly to the entrance of the museum. Surprisingly, Travis calmed down and entered the museum without a whimper.

My mother motioned over her shoulder. The small crowd was staring at us. They were talking in low tones, but I heard one woman say as we entered the building, "What were those women doing to that child?" I looked at my mother, and we both began laughing. Josh began giggling, and soon Travis was laughing, too. I put Travis's hand in my mother's and walked back to the group of people.

I reached in my pocket and pulled out a card that said, "My student has autism." On the other side of the card was a brief description of autism. I handed the card to the group.

I had decided when I first began taking my students with autism into the community that I needed a way to educate those with whom we came in contact. This was especially important because most of the children with autism I knew did not appear to have a disability. I had heard way too many comments such as, "Why can't she control that child?" or "Look at that brat." I had found the cards at a national conference on autism and carried them with me when I was out and about.

Later, as we were leaving the museum, a young woman approached us. She had been the vocal member of the group that watched our hedge adventure. She apologized for her rudeness, and thanked me for taking the time to help her understand.

My mother and I tried to figure out what had frightened Travis. She thought it was the large statue of a dinosaur that they had passed. I thought it might have been the noon whistle that blew. Perhaps it was a combination of the two. In any event, we took another route to the car, and Travis was fine.

Conclusion

The autism spectrum is a kaleidoscope of ever changing patterns and colors, making the education of a person on the spectrum an ongoing challenge. Just as you and I are individuals, those on the autism spectrum are uniquely and equally different.

As an educator, you will meet many individuals with autism. You must get to know the total person, autism and all, before you can begin to color his or her world. In the educational environment you must continually revise, refine, and abandon methods and strategies.

The color of autism is never monochromatic. It's palette ranges from subtle pastels to splashes of intense primary colors. Students with autism will challenge you, they will frustrate you, but ultimately they will enrich your life.

Printed in the USA
CPSIA information can be obtained
at www.ICGtesting.com
JSHW082212140824
68134JS00014B/584